FULL SPEED AHEAD

Be Driven by Your Dream to Maximize
Your Success and Live the Life
You Want

JOYCE WEISS, CSP

Full Speed Ahead

Joyce Weiss
E-mail: JoyceWeiss@aol.com
Copyright © 2002 by Joyce Weiss
www.joyceweiss.com
ISBN 0-938716-44-1

Published by
POSSIBILITY PRESS
E-mail: posspress@aol.com

Manufactured in the United States of America

Other Books by *Possibility Press*

No Excuse!...Key Principles for Balancing Life and Achieving Success
No Excuse! I'm Doing It...How to Do Whatever It Takes to Make It Happen
No Excuse! The Workbook...Your Companion to the Book to
Help You Live the "No Excuse!" Lifestyle
Reject Me—I Love It!...21 Secrets for Turning Rejection Into Direction
If They Say No, Just Say NEXT!...24 Secrets for Going Through
the Noes to Get to the Yeses
The Electronic Dream...Essential Ingredients for Growing a
People Business in an e-Commerce World
Time And Money.com...Create Wealth by Profiting from
the Explosive Growth of E-Commerce
Are You Living Your Dream?...How to Create Wealth and
Live the Life You Want...You Can Do It!
If It Is To Be, It's Up To Me...How to Develop the Attitude of a
Winner *and* Become a Leader
Get A GRIP On Your Dream...12 Ways to Squeeze More Success Out of Your Goals
Are You Fired Up?...How to Ignite Your Enthusiasm and
Make Your Dreams Come True
Dream Achievers...50 Powerful Stories of People Just Like You
Who Became Leaders in Network Marketing
Focus On Your Dream...How to Turn Your Dreams and Goals Into Reality
SOAR To The Top...Rise Above the Crowd and Fly Away to Your Dream
In Business And In Love...How Couples Can Successfully
Run a Marriage-Based Business
Schmooze 'Em Or Lose 'Em...How to Build High-Touch
Relationships in a High-Tech World
SCORE Your Way To Success...How to Get Your Life on Target
What Choice Do I Have?...21 Choice Ways to Achieve the Results You Want
in Your Work and in Your Life
Dump The Debt And Get Free...A Realistic and Sensible Plan to
Eliminate Debt and Build Wealth in the 21st Century
Congratulations! You're A Millionaire!...The Secrets to Selling Your Way to a Fortune
Brighten Your Day With Self-Esteem...How to Empower, Energize
and Motivate Yourself to a Richer, Fuller, More Rewarding Life
Naked People Won't Help You...Keep Your Cool, Capture the Confidence,
And Conquer the Fear of Public Speaking

Tapes by *Possibility Press*

Turning Rejection Into Direction...A Roundtable Discussion With
Network Marketing Independent Business Owners

Dedication

To my parents, Joseph and Sara Morris, for encouraging me to march to a different drummer. Thanks for the trust and love you give to me, and the strength to help others find their own magic— the tremendous potential that lies within them.

Acknowledgments

To my husband, Jerry, my dearest friend and business mentor, who always encourages me as my multi-faceted career continues to grow.

To my children, Ron, Wendy, Jodi, and Brian, and grandchildren, who give me the greatest stories to share. I'm very pleased with your strength and internal drive which inspires me!

To my sister, Marcia, and brother-in-law, Irving, for being my personal cheerleaders. Thanks for taking my continuous phone calls as you helped me to create the book's title.

I love all of you very much, and I hope I have made as much of an impact on you as you have made on me! Your support and energy are always a part of me.

To my marketing director, Rita Jones, whose dedication, work ethic, and warmth keep the business running smoothly. Thanks for challenging me daily and for telling me things I *need* to hear.

To my editors and publisher, thanks for your talent and many hours of debate and dedication to this project.

Finally, to my audiences, clients, and loyal friends who kept asking me to write a book. There would be no book without your input and encouragement. Thank you for sharing your challenges and successes with me. You have made my career a total joy.

To all of you who want to do more than just survive. *Full Speed Ahead* is for people who are striving to achieve their personal best. Enjoy!

Contents

Prologue
Ladies and Gentlemen, Start Your Engines

"Freedom is never granted; it is won."
A. Philip Randolph

Far too many people are content with merely surviving—just getting by. To find true happiness and success, you need to do more than that in your business or profession, as well as in your personal life. You need to *thrive*. Let your dream drive you to overcome any obstacles that get in your way. Challenge yourself so you can grow and reach your potential.

To be ultimately successful and create the life you want, express yourself and take action. You can't be successful alone, so appreciate and accept the differences in the people you need to associate with. Develop a dynamic team where everyone pulls together—driven by their dreams, their reasons why.

Life constantly provides us with opportunities, typically disguised as challenges, for growing and becoming. Pursuing your dream fuels this process, while failure and success both provide powerful lessons along the way. Life can be a magical experience when you are open-minded and accept all the challenges it gives you. After all, growing *through* challenges offers you excellent opportunities to reach more of your potential.

As you move on, you'll discover even more challenges that can provide you with even greater opportunities for growth. The fact is, you can grow only when you squarely meet and overcome more obstacles. This is how you get to the next level of your personal development, which is the key to your success in all areas of your life! As George S. Patton, Jr. once said, "Accept the challenges so that you may feel the exhilaration of victory."

This book features stories from my workshop participants, as well as my own personal experiences, which illustrate how the human spirit can accelerate through challenges and go *full speed ahead!* Proven practical exercises will help you recognize the skills you already have to excel.

You'll also learn about the tools you need to fine-tune and add to those skills, so you can make your dream a reality. When you want to accelerate to the next level, in any arena of life, shift your thinking and behavior into the next higher gear. *You cannot solve a problem on the same level it was created.* You need to learn, grow, and take different actions to create new and better results.

This book can help you excel, and achieve your goals and dreams, by suggesting options to assist you through those challenges. Then you can proceed *full speed ahead* to achieve your personal best and get in the passing lane on the road to your dream. Top performers realize that their best can always get better. They know that constant improvement is a habit for excellence—at home, in business, and in all areas of life.

I hope this book helps you achieve more success and happiness. Every day is a fresh new beginning—a chance to do whatever it takes to get closer to living your dream. Get into the driver's seat and grab the wheel of your high-performance vehicle. Start your engine, put it in gear, and "put the pedal to the metal"—*become driven by your dream and go full speed ahead to attain it!*

Introduction
Revving Up for Success

"If a man does not keep pace with his companions, perhaps it is because he hears a different drummer. Let him step to the music which he hears, however measured or far away."
Henry David Thoreau

Have you ever said any of the following things to yourself?

♦ I'm so stressed-out, I just don't know what to *do* anymore—I'm stuck in neutral.

♦ If one more negative thing happens to me today, I'll *scream*.

♦ My boss just doesn't understand *me, or my job*. I have to do more with less and I just can't take it anymore!

♦ My family expects too much of me. I just can't keep up. I'm really feeling like a doormat.

♦ Work used to be fun. I used to enjoy my job. But these days I'm just putting in the time at work—living for the weekends. I wouldn't bother going in at all if I didn't have bills. I can't wait until I retire!

♦ There's no time in my life for *me*. I'm on a treadmill, going nowhere fast, and I don't know how to get off.

♦ I did everything my parents, teachers, supervisors, and managers told me to do, and my life *still* isn't working.

It's no secret that our workaday world is often like a pressure cooker. To think about all the things that can cause stress is mind-boggling. So what are you supposed to do? Try not to think about it? As you may have experienced, that doesn't work. If you shy away from achieving your rightful share of success and happiness in this world, you merely survive—rather than grow and thrive. And as I'm sure you've observed, all too many people are doing *just that*—"grinding it out."

The aim of this book is to help you gain the control you need to excel in all areas of your life. It's to help you get "revved up" for success, so you can make your dreams come true. Completing the exercises and implementing the action plan at the end of each chapter will help you put more joy, fun, and creativity into your life—so you can better enjoy the journey of your success. You'll learn ways to reach your potential to create the kind of life you want. The vision of that life lies within you—maybe deep within you—but it *is* there.

All the great men and women of history, and of our time, are no better than you and me. They've simply found a way to reach deep within themselves and generate the courage, wisdom, and strength to create their place in history.

Whenever I walk on the beautiful beaches of the world, I look at the powerful waves and compare them to us. Like the mighty oceans, we *all* have magnificent potential. Treasures and mysteries lie within our depths just as they do at the bottom of the ocean.

You were born with everything you need to be the person you want to be, to do what you want to do, and to have what you want to have. All these things add up to your dream. And you have more control and choices than you may think. For example, you can choose to get financially free, if you want. It's up to you. Your life is simply the sum of the choices you make every day.

In my workshops I love to use this catchy little phrase: *"The magic inside you is no hocus pocus. Set your goals and you create the focus."* I define magic as a process to unveil the potential that resides and operates within each of us. As American writer Ralph Waldo Emerson said, "What lies behind us and what lies before us are tiny matters compared to what lies within us."

You may be saying to yourself, "Yeah, yeah, this all sounds good, but how can I make it work for me? How can I overcome my daily challenges and add excitement, joy, and creativity to my life? How can I break free from daily routines and self-limiting boundaries? How can I get beyond just making a living—to creating the life I want? How can I achieve my personal best and make my dream a reality?"

To create the life you want, I encourage you to write in a notebook or day planner "keeper ideas" that you want to remember. Be as specific as possible. Use people's names, names of places, brand names, times, and such. The more descriptive you are, the more likely you'll achieve the results you want. Keep your notes with you and refer to them throughout the day as you develop strategies to help you go *full speed ahead*. People who win focus on success-generating ideas, and don't allow themselves to be distracted by anything else.

As you develop your personal action plan, use your immediate keeper ideas to help you focus on your goals and gain more control over your life. You'll be better able to more clearly determine what you need to do to make things happen, so you can achieve your dream.

As a professional speaker, I have the opportunity to interview hundreds of people at my workshops. Along the way, they've shared various insights about how they faced and overcame their challenges. Some worked for the government, some were educators, some were leaders, while still others were on the front lines. Some were in corporate settings; others were at home. I'll be sharing some of their tremendous ideas that I have found along the way. I'll also be sharing ideas with you that I've learned from my resources and life experiences.

You may already use some of these ideas. Experiment to determine what works best for you. And, as you use these ideas, you'll learn what you need to do to be your personal best. Your life can be better. The choices you make every day determine what kind of life you live. You already have many answers. Use this book as a catalyst to help you discover solutions that are right for you. Then you can put more joy, fun, and creativity into your life and find the happiness and satisfaction you deserve.

Remember the wise words of Abraham Lincoln, *"Always bear in mind that your own resolution to succeed is more important than any one thing."* And American inventory Charles Kettering wrote, "You will never stub your toe standing still. The faster you go, the more chance there is of stubbing your toe, but the more chance you have of getting somewhere."

Now let's get revved up for success and move *full speed ahead*. Be driven by your dream to maximize your success and live the life you want.

Chapter 1

Gaining Control—Put Yourself in the Driver's Seat

"No man is free who is not master of himself."
Epictetus

What Could Be Holding You Back?

Let's begin by discussing some things you may or may not be doing that could be negatively affecting your ability to be successful. The question is, "What are you doing, or failing to do, that could be holding you back from living your dream?"

Here are some examples for you to consider:

♦ Do you have a negative attitude?

♦ Are you watching the negative news on TV, listening to it on the radio, or reading it in the newspaper?

♦ Are you in the daily habit of reading personal development books that are helping you grow as a person?

♦ Are you associating with negative-thinking people who are attempting to steal your dream? (By the way, they can only do that if you let them.)

♦ Are you meeting and making friends with new positive-thinking people? Are you regularly associating with winners?

♦ Do you look for the good in people and situations?

- Are you committed to doing whatever it takes to make your dream a reality? Are you just talking the talk, or are you walking the walk?

- Do you dislike your job, yet fail to do what is necessary to move on and create the life you really want?

- Do you find yourself constantly discussing sickness or problems i.e., focusing on the negative with people who are basically stuck in life?

- Are you investing in yourself and your business or profession through continuing education activities like going to seminars and listening to educational and motivational audiocassette tapes?

- Are you in close communication with a forward-thinking person who is a mentor to you?

- Are you bogged down with debt, living beyond your means, and not doing anything about it?

- Do you have personal and professional goals?

- Are you making each day count by focusing on your dream, and doing something daily that moves you closer to it? Or, are you just busy, doing everyday maintenance activities that aren't productive? Are you just spending time, rather than *investing* it in your future?

What else would you add to this list?

Go from Reactive to Proactive

How can you move from being reactive, i.e., having a "knee-jerk" reaction (virtually automatic) to what you encounter day-to-day, to being proactive? Do you take the initiative and follow through with planned action to change a situation you don't like? You need to keep negative input out of your life as much as possible since it saps your valuable energy. Turn adversity into an opportunity for growth and positive change.

Most people seem to waste their lives complaining about challenges that simply come as a result of being alive and interacting with others and the environment. This is an easy thing to do. Yet, it gets us nowhere except further entrenched in the situation we don't want.

You get what you focus on. So you need to focus on what you want, not on what you don't want.

Trade negativity for positive energy, so you can get beyond the challenges, and create the life you want. Then, if someone asks "How are you?" say, "I'm excited and making my dreams come true," instead of saying "Same old, same old," or just, "Okay." What's your response been lately? How could you upgrade it? You could say, "Great!" Break out in a big smile and they'll probably wonder what you're up to!

Have you had enough negativity? Take a deep breath, then exhale—forcing all negative thoughts from your body. Now inhale deeply, filling your lungs with oxygen and the fresh air of positive energy.

Be a "Goodfinder"

Always look for the positive—be a goodfinder. Give people sincere compliments regularly and look for the good in any situations that may arise. If you're already doing this, my hat goes off to you and to all the eternal optimists who are reading this book. However, most people need to exert more effort in this area to transition into being a goodfinder.

Some of us have had more negative programming than others. You may be asking yourself, "How can I grow and stay fired up about my dream in such a negative-thinking world?"

Here are five strategies to help you be a goodfinder as you deal with the daily challenges of life:

1. **Put your thoughts into action!** Take positive action every day, doing whatever it takes to realize your dreams and goals.
2. **Accept responsibility for your decisions and actions.** Take responsibility rather than blaming others. You'll feel and be more in control.
3. **Accept and appreciate the differences in others instead of judging them.** Be thankful we're not all alike!
4. **Welcome the challenge of change!** Prepare yourself for change—it's an inevitable part of life.
5. **Attitudes are contagious—is yours worth catching?** Maintain a positive attitude regardless of what happens in the world around you.

Strategy 1—*Put Your Thoughts into Action*

We all face challenges in life such as health issues, having a job we dislike, being in debt, investing our time wisely, and the like. Just because certain people *look* like they don't have challenges, don't be fooled! Are you letting life's challenges keep you stuck in situations where you're unhappy? Remember, *you* choose how you respond to situations. Some have learned to carefully respond while others just react without thinking of the possible consequences. How about you?

Seventeenth century French philosopher and writer Voltaire compared life to a game in which each player must accept the cards he was dealt. Once in hand, he or she alone can decide how to play those cards to win the game.

Shakespeare said, "Life breaks all of us. Some of us get stronger at the breaks." Be one who gets stronger and helps others do the same.

You can choose to dwell on your problems or *focus on the solutions* and get on with your life. Take time to mourn a loss—a loved one who has died, a job lost to downsizing, a marriage torn apart, or any other significant change in your life. You need a certain amount of time to heal. It is important to deal with the stages of loss, but then *move on*. Don't dwell on the past and use it as an excuse not to create the life you want.

Do what you need to do. Some people are so busy just *thinking* about what they need in order to live their dream that they don't *do* what is necessary to make it happen.

For example, an independent business owner or other professional person may believe they're taking action, i.e., building their business or career, when they attend training sessions, continuing education or motivational seminars, conventions, and other activities related to the vehicle they've chosen to drive to their dream. They socialize with the other attendees, learn new things, and get excited about reaching their goals and dreams. That's great and it's definitely a key part of going *full speed ahead*. However, a lot of people have just become motivational and educational junkies. And, amazingly, they often don't understand why they're not more successful!

So what can they do? First, they certainly need to maintain their level of enthusiasm and gain knowledge. Keep listening to motivational and educational tapes every day and associating with other positive-thinking people who are learning and growing. Second, they need to firmly put themselves in the driver's seat of their vehicle and *take* action with what they've learned. Nothing happens until they *do* something that moves them forward.

Get into and participate in a success system. Learn from the leaders. Put your pedal to the metal and get into action! Leave the past behind. It's over and done with. Get in the driver's seat and make it happen for yourself and your family. Others are doing it and you can too!

Strategy 2—*Accept Responsibility*

You have the ability to choose your responses to challenging situations. *You* choose whether you live a boring, unfulfilled, miserable life of surviving day to day, or a life full of joy, contentment, growth, and financial freedom.

Some people blame their parents, boss, mate, or business associates for the way things are. They don't accept responsibility for their own lives. They've adopted a victim mentality. A timeless wisdom from the 16th century says, "Grant me the serenity to accept the things I cannot change, the courage to change the things I can, and the wisdom to know the difference." We *all* need to keep this simple, yet profound, thought close to our hearts.

Some people find it easy to just blame and complain. They need to shift into a positive gear. Here's a simple, effective question to ask yourself or someone else who's stuck in neutral— "Now that I (or you) recognize the problem, what am I (or you) going to do about it?" Be a leader and show others that *you* are self-responsible, and encourage them to do the same. Remember, all change begins with you—*lead by your example!*

After I earned my masters degree in guidance and counseling, many people called me to complain about their mate or their job. At first I just listened and empathized. Then I realized that many of them were bright, loving people who had been complaining for years, but never made any changes! They were "spinning their wheels," going nowhere—like a gerbil running in a caged wheel. I began to respond with, "I've listened and you have a legitimate complaint. Now my question to you is, 'What are you going to do about it?'" A lot of their phone calls ceased. It was no longer fun for the complainers, who were used to crying on my shoulder. They needed to look to *themselves* for solutions!

As a spouse, friend, business associate, boss, leader, parent, or in any other role you may have assumed, be sure to tell the people, especially those who are important to you, what they *need* to hear, not just what they *want* to hear! Do it with kindness—care about the person. Share how you feel about their behavior, without verbally lashing out at them with cutting words that could negatively affect their self-esteem. It takes courage and you can do it.

Once, while presenting a workshop to a Fortune 500 company, management told me what they tell all new employees. They suggest that new staffers look at constructive feedback as a gift, and not take it personally and become defensive or insecure about it. What an incredible message!

Accept responsibility for your actions, and *move on* when you feel stuck. These are two important things to do when dealing with challenges.

Strategy 3—*Accept and Appreciate the Differences in Others*

Learning to accept and appreciate differences in others, without judging them, is another vital lesson. You might be thinking, "I'm a fair person; I don't judge people." Look at the following list. Have you ever caught yourself saying these things?

- ◆ "You should have known better."
- ◆ "I can't believe you did that."
- ◆ "Why did you quit your job when you had all those benefits?"
- ◆ "How could you possibly date *that* person?"
- ◆ "What do you mean you don't smoke?"
- ◆ "Chill out and join the party."
- ◆ "Tofu? How disgusting!"
- ◆ "What would the neighbors think?"

These are examples of subtle and not so subtle ways of judging others. When words like should, could, or why creep into the conversation, look out! These words shout, "Be like me, because different from me is wrong!" Pay close attention to your words. Strive to become nonjudgmental in all your communications. Remember the importance of accepting and appreciating the differences in others.

Strategy 4—*Welcome the Challenge of Change!*

Change is inevitable in this fast-paced world. Some major changes in life relate to health, jobs, business, relocation, a new boss or co-worker, death of a loved one, or the breakup of a close relationship. Minor changes could be the weather, traffic, your hairstyle, and new eyeglasses or contact lenses. These minor changes may seem insignificant, but nonetheless, such things are likely to affect us every day, in one way or another.

Some believe that life just happens to us, failing to understand that it is a cause-and-effect world. Things happen for a reason. Some things are truly out of our control. But we can control our attitude and look for the positive. If we look hard enough, we may notice how the change occurred. It may be the result of poor communications, or something else we had a role in.

French novelist Victor Hugo once wrote, "The future has several names. For the weak, it is impossible. For the faint-hearted, it is the unknown. For the thoughtful and valiant, it is ideal." And as Will Rogers, noted American author, actor, and down-home philosopher, said, "Those were great old days! But darn it, any old days are great old days, even the tough ones. After they are over you can look back with great memories." So much change has occurred, frequently due to new technology, in such a relatively short time. Change is ever-present!

Participants in my workshops sometimes complain when I ask them to change seats and find new partners for an exercise. They groan, "Do we have to?" or "I like my space!" These activities challenge their comfort zones. Yet others thrive on change and love to be paired with new people. Such courageous people face the fear of change and find it exciting!

You might as well be prepared for change. It's going to happen—even if you're not prepared! And flexible people are more likely to succeed.

A classic example of flexibility is found in the popular Aesop fable, *The Oak and the Reeds*. A proud oak tree grew on the banks of a stream. For a hundred years it withstood the buffeting of the winds. Then one day a violent storm knocked the great oak to the ground with a mighty crash and blew it into the swollen river, which carried it toward the sea. The oak tree came to rest on the shore, where some reeds were growing. The tree was amazed to see the reeds standing upright, not bent at all from the strong winds.

"How did you manage to weather that terrible storm?" the Tree asked. "I have stood up against many a storm, but this one was too strong for me." "That's just it," replied the Reed. "All these years you have stubbornly pitted your great strength against the wind. You were too proud to yield a little. I, on the other hand, knowing my weakness, didn't resist. The harder the wind blew, the more I let go of my pride and bent, so here I am!"

Start with a little change at a time. Alter just a few small habits daily. For example, listen to a continuing education tape that motivates you, instead of the radio—as you travel to and from work. Much of what appears on TV and in the newspapers won't help you succeed anyway. It's just entertainment. Take 15-20 minutes each day, when you would normally watch TV or read the newspaper, and invest that time in yourself by reading a personal development book. Invest your time in activities that will take you closer to your goals. (If you haven't set your goals yet, now is a great time! Go ahead and write them down.)

Go out to lunch with a new friend or different co-worker. You may even develop a relationship that'll lead to teaming up to achieve a common goal. You won't know unless you venture out a little. How about taking a brisk walk at lunch and listening to a positive tape as you do? You'll feel invigorated mentally and physically!

Raise the standards you've set for your own behavior when you want to change. It's time to modify the limiting belief, "I've always done it like that." *If you want some things to change in your life, you need to change some things in your life!* This means creating some new success-generating habits. That makes sense, doesn't it? Yet a lot of people are on automatic, always in a reactive mode. They don't seem to understand this simple truth!

You cannot change a habit simply by talking about it. You need to *take action!* If you sincerely want your life to improve, you need to adjust your daily routines accordingly. If you have something else that you need to do on a weekend when you would normally work, ask for that weekend off. Give your boss enough notice so he or she can adjust the schedule accordingly. Make it as easy as possible for your boss to say yes. Make an agreement with a co-worker to switch weekends in advance!

Each time I want to make a change in a certain aspect of my behavior, this is what I do—I put 10 pennies in my right pocket in the morning. When I notice I'm using a new skill or breaking an old habit, I move a penny to my left pocket. At the end of the day I count the pennies in each pocket and review the actions I took to change my habit. This is an easy exercise. The results are obvious, and the rewards are uplifting. You continue to build confidence in your ability to get the results you want. I stopped using the expression "you know" by doing this. It works!

One of the best examples you can give future generations, your children, co-workers, business associates, and other people you deal with is to constantly upgrade your skills. Keep learning and always be flexible. When you experience change, and you surely will, you'll then be like the flexible reed rather than the rigid oak. Here is an example.

When my children were young I met a little girl named Susie, who was afraid of most men. Since she was starting nursery school, her mother took her to meet the other mothers and children in the carpool. She wanted to prepare her so she wouldn't be afraid. Wouldn't you know it, on the first day of school, the mother charged with driving got sick and sent her husband to pick up the children! Even though Susie's mother had done her best to prepare her, Susie still had to confront her fear. We all need to learn to adapt to change. Susie surely did and, as a result, she overcame her fear.

When you find yourself doing well and are satisfied in a personal or business-related situation, challenge yourself by asking, "How can I do better?" People lose out when they rest on their laurels, thinking they have achieved their goals and don't need to improve their skills and habits. They're just fooling themselves. It's so much more fun and productive to dream bigger and set new, more challenging goals! This causes us to stretch and grow. So keep pushing "the edge of the envelope."

Strategy 5—*Attitude Is Contagious—Is Yours Worth Catching?*

When you observe successful people as they deal with their challenges, you'll notice a common theme which can be summed up in one simple word, the A word—Attitude. These people are consistently monitoring and upgrading their attitude. They have or develop a positive outlook—no matter *what* they're experiencing. They know every challenge has something beneficial within it.

Having a positive attitude is the main key to your success personally and professionally. Anyone who believes they can change a negative attitude into a positive one, and puts this idea into practice daily, is bound to have a happier, more fulfilling life. No matter how skilled you are, without a terrific attitude, you are in for a bumpy ride on your road of success.

One of my favorite movies is *Forrest Gump*. The story covers the life of a 30-year-old man with an intelligence quotient (IQ) of 75. His mother, regardless of his low IQ, told Forrest, "You can be anything you want to be." When Forrest Gump's girlfriend asked him, "What are you going to be?" Forrest innocently replied, "Aren't I going to be me?"

Douglas Malloch, in his poem, *Be The Best Of Whatever You Are,* wrote, "If you can't be a highway, then be a trail. If you can't be the sun, be a star. It isn't by size that you win or you fail. Be the best of whatever you are!" He drove *full speed ahead* to his dream.

Rudy Ruettiger comes to mind when I think of people who achieve their personal best because they *never* give up on their dreams. Why is his story so special? As a child, he had a dream—to play football for a certain prestigious school. Rudy graduated from high school with terrible grades and had very little athletic ability. He seemed to be a most unlikely candidate! Family and friends laughed at him for stubbornly holding on to his dream. Yet Rudy had a vision and decided to fight for the right to play football for this university.

Rudy's next few years consisted of working with his father and brother in the steel mills because "The Ruettigers don't go to college." Then Rudy decided to attend a junior (two-year) college. There he met a priest who promised Rudy he would pay his tuition if he worked hard and received excellent grades. Why did that happen? Rudy was committed—that's why! It was no accident.

Rudy consistently worked toward his dream and was finally accepted to his dream school—the University of Notre Dame in the U.S. He tried out for the football team again and again, and was always rejected. The coach thought Rudy was too short and lacked the necessary skills to play on the team. But this didn't dampen Rudy's enthusiasm; with all his heart, he wanted to play football! So Rudy, keeping an optimistic attitude, despite the odds, persistently showed up for every tryout session.

Finally, the coach relented and let him join the team. The coach had never met a player who wanted something as passionately as Rudy wanted to be a part of his team.

However, Rudy still had some roadblocks to overcome. During the football season, the coach never allowed Rudy to play in a regular game! He had only been permitted to play during practice sessions. In the last game of the season, however, the players convinced the coach to allow Rudy to play. As a result, he made a tremendous play that actually won the game—the *only* game that Rudy was ever allowed to play!

Rudy's teammates respected his perseverance and work ethic. At the end of the game they carried him, their new hero, off the field on their shoulders as the crowd roared "Rudy, Rudy, Rudy..." over and over again. This happened in 1976—the year Rudy graduated from Notre Dame. And since then, no other player has been carried off the field in such a victorious manner.

What an inspiring story for all of us. Here was a young man who stood tall against the odds and wouldn't take *no* for an answer. My daughter, Wendy, introduced me to the tremendously uplifting movie, *Rudy*, and to the novel based on Rudy's experiences, which was written by James Ellison. Rudy, now a popular professional speaker, also wrote the book, *Rudy's Rules*.

Excellence Is a Habit

Greek philosopher Aristotle wrote, "We are what we repeatedly do. Excellence, then, is not an act, but a habit." British writer Somerset Maugham penned, "If you refuse to accept anything but the best, you often get it."

Find your special uniqueness. And stay away from negative-thinking people—dreamstealers, who put you down and try to stop you from reaching your dreams and fulfilling your potential. Again, participating in a continuing education and motivation program is key. Ask other successful people in your business or profession to give you guidance, be a mentor, and recommend some books and tapes that'll help you to learn and have a positive attitude.

Associate with dreambuilders and other people who support you and your dreams. Find other people at motivational seminars who are also excited about life and moving on. Also, ask your mentor for their suggestions of seminars you could attend. Obtain dates and times, and schedule them into your day planner or datebook so you can plan ahead.

We need to stop saying "I can't" and "It's impossible"—words which only serve to limit our creativity. They just promote failure. Pogo, the cartoon character, may be right when he says, "I have found the worst enemy and it is me." Be your own best friend, rather than your own worst enemy. French emperor and military strategist Napoleon once said, "Impossible is a word to be found only in the dictionary of fools." Be a "can do" possibility-oriented person—that's the attitude that wins, no matter what the odds may be.

Playwright Neil Simon said, "Don't listen to those who say it's not done that way. Maybe it's not, but maybe you'll do it anyway. Don't listen to those who say you're taking too big a chance. Michelangelo would have painted the floor of the Sistine

Chapel if he had listened to average people, and it would surely have been rubbed out by now." For example, if someone puts you down, be courteous, and let it go. There are always naysayers—those who are jealous and quick to criticize. As the old saying goes, "There are no statues erected to critics." You need to do what's right for you, even if others don't understand or agree.

We have many choices in how to live our lives. Some choose to live surrounded by negative-thinking people. Others choose to associate with forward-thinking people and grow and become their personal best. Winners create the future they want, while others wait endlessly, hoping opportunity will knock at their door and give them an exciting life!

People who invest time in reading about personal growth, then use what they learn, create their futures! Optimists realize they have options and they find solutions to their challenges. They see the opportunities that life provides. They know they need to be flexible and continue growing to go *full speed ahead.*

Think about your challenges. What is your greatest obstacle? Is it fear? What is the biggest mistake you ever made? Is it giving up, rather than doing whatever it takes to achieve your goals? What is your greatest weakness? Is it finding fault with yourself and others? What do you like best about yourself? Is it your uniqueness? What is your greatest gift? Is it forgiveness?

And what is your greatest day? It's today! Today is the *only* day you can take action and experience your life. So make it a great experience!

As Henry David Thoreau once said, "Events, circumstances, and situations have their origins in ourselves. They spring from seeds we have sown."

Now Implement the *Full Speed Ahead* Action Plan...

Get a piece of paper and answer the following eight questions:

1. What situations do I find stressful in my profession, job or business, and in my personal life?
2. If I feel upset, how do I typically react?
3. What specific upcoming situations do I anticipate may be stressful?

4. Which people cause me to experience stressful feelings—at my job or business and in my personal life?

5. What things do these people do, or don't do, that I find unpleasant?

6. What can I do to prepare myself more effectively for these situations (avoid them, change my behavior, or accept them)?

7. Have I put myself in the driver's seat in these situations? Or, have I allowed someone else to take the wheel? If so, who? How can I take responsibility next time?

8. How do I approach these experiences? Do I tell the story as if I'm a victim or in the driver's seat? How can I take full responsibility for my behavior? Do so with each situation in #1 now.

BATTERY

Chapter 2

Stress—Recharge Your Battery by Channeling Stress into Positive Energy

*"Even if you're on the right track, you'll get run over
if you just sit there."*
Will Rogers

Stress Can Benefit You!

Have you ever wondered how you made it through the day? Everyone has their own daily challenges and situations that cause stress. You simply can't avoid it. Even babies have stress. Have you ever heard infants cry for milk when they're hungry? Tell me that's not stressful.

Your attitude about stress and how you handle it will largely determine what effect it has on you. Would you like to feel more energized and gain more control over your busy life?

In ancient times, the wind meant great trouble for human beings. It constantly blew down their structures, put out their fires, and generally, was a real challenge. People realized that the mighty winds were inevitable—a force of nature that could not be stopped—so they began to *deal with it*. As they learned more about it, they discovered they could use the power of the wind for windmills and sailboats. Today, we are finding new ways to channel the wind into a force for positive change. *You could think of the stress in your life as the wind.* This chapter teaches you how to channel that stress into positive energy.

Many people need more balance in their lives. This is especially true for those who live in fast-paced environments. The participants in my stress management workshops often vent their frustrations about not enjoying their work and not having enough time for their families or themselves. Some people are so busy making a living that they don't have time to make a life!

What is your life like? Where are *you* going? How are you using your time? Are you just limping along? Are you sitting by the side of the road, broken down? Or, are you traveling on the road of success—*full speed ahead?*

What if You Had to Deplete Your Bank Account Every Day?

Picture the following scenario: Your bank puts $86,400 into your checking account each morning. You're not allowed to carry a balance from one day to the next. Every day you'd lose whatever you failed to spend or invest that day. What would you do? Would you withdraw and use every cent each day?

Do you realize you have such an account? It's called *time.* Every morning it credits you with 86,400 seconds. It carries over no balances. It allows no overdrafts. You begin each day with a new deposit. Each night it burns the records of that day. If you fail to use each day's deposit, the loss is yours. There is no going back. There is no borrowing against tomorrow. You can live only in the present on today's balance.

Use each day to achieve the utmost in health, happiness, and success. Remember our earlier statement: *Most people are so busy making a living they don't have time to make a life.* So, make each day count! As Ralph Waldo Emerson said, "With the past, I have nothing to do; nor with the future. I live now."

What Is Stress?

My favorite definition of stress is—a state of emotion or time when you don't take care of your own needs. It doesn't matter if you are at work, at home, or somewhere else. If you ignore your own needs, stress or displeasure results. Some people internalize these feelings. Later their stress comes out as anger or physical symptoms, like stomach pains and backaches. Many people waste too much time on control busters—feelings that zap energy and rob time. The five control busters you'll learn about in this chapter are:

1. *Fear*—how to feel fear, and work to overcome it and not let it get in the way of your achieving your goals.
2. *Worry*—how to eliminate worry so you can enjoy today and have more energy to invest in your future.
3. *Failure*—how to use it as a temporary setback which teaches you valuable lessons.
4. *Adversity*—how opportunity comes from challenging times.
5. *People Pleasing*—how to respond rather than react to other's agendas.

Ask yourself these two important questions: Am I living the kind of life I want? And, am I taking care of my needs, as well as investing time with positive-thinking people who support me and my dreams and goals?

Remember: *The magic inside you is no hocus pocus. Set your goals and you create the focus.* All the answers to life's riddles are within your own heart. You already know how to gain the control you need to move toward your dream and enjoy the journey. How about going *full speed ahead?* You can fine-tune and learn more along the way. If you wait until someday, when you believe you'll have no obstacles, you will probably wait forever. Someday usually turns into never.

I use the following exercise to open my workshops on stress management. I ask participants to gather into small groups and think of ways to show how they are working too hard on their jobs. Some of their comical answers follow. You are working too hard if:

♦ You rush home from your 9 to 5 job just in time to catch the 11 o'clock news.
♦ You wake up at 6 a.m. and dress for work before you realize it's your day off.

- ◆ You answer your home phone with your employer's name.
- ◆ You buy new underwear because you don't have time to do your laundry.
- ◆ Your dog or cat doesn't recognize you.

With some clues to identify whether you are working your job too hard, let's discuss each of the five control busters that may be stopping you from living a more successful, fulfilling, and happy life. Thousands of wonderful people I have spoken with over the years have shared with me how they sabotage themselves. Are you sabotaging yourself as well because you've spent too much time on control busters?

Fear—the first control buster. We are born with only two fears—the fear of falling and the fear of loud noises. All other fears are learned. We may be accepting what negative-thinking people are telling us. We may also be putting negative thoughts and messages into our own minds. Fear is based on a lack of knowledge and confidence in ourselves that we can handle whatever challenges we encounter. It also comes from a lack of confidence in other people. You may need to remove this road-block to continue on your road of success. Look at the word "fear" and simply think of it as an acronym:

F = false
E = evidence
A = appearing
R = real

So what can you do to face fear? What do you need to do to be successful in all areas of your life? My workshop participants tell me how they face fear and fight it. They admit it's a challenge. But nonetheless, it *is* possible.

Some people, when faced with doing something they're afraid to do, take a detour into "What If" land. They may say they want to meet new people to share their company's products and services, or perhaps an opportunity. Yet they ask, "What if they say no?" or "What if I forget to tell them something?"

If they focus on the negative, these people sound timid and unconvinced in their approach. Instead they need to be optimistic, and understand that it's okay if someone says no. We all need to do the best we can to share what we have to offer and to meet other people's needs. Then it's up to the prospect or associate what choice they make—*their behavior is about them.*

If we forget to tell that person something, it's no big deal. This just gives us a great chance to interact with that person again. So don't concern yourself with what ifs. Fear is simply a false belief that you won't be able to handle a particular outcome.

Shad Helmstetter says in his book *What To Say When You Talk To Yourself,* "As much as 88 percent of what you tell yourself may be working *against* you!" Be careful what you say to yourself! Do you label yourself as a failure, or too old, or too uneducated, or too stupid to succeed? Are you constantly telling yourself that negative things are going to happen to you?

You need to silence the internal noise inside your mind—any negative self-talk that erodes your attitude and self-confidence. You have the power and control to lead a calmer, stronger life. Others have done it and you can too. Train yourself to eliminate fearful and destructive thoughts and replace them with positive, constructive ones. Fear doesn't help you overcome tomorrow's challenges, and it can surely ruin today's happiness. So what good is it? Perhaps the answer is, "Fear can show us where we need to grow."

When I tell people that I give over a hundred workshops and speeches each year before thousands of people, the typical responses are, "I could never do that" or "I would love to speak, but I'm so afraid." Have you ever felt that way before making a presentation, or sharing your products or services? Fear of public speaking is common for many people. Other fears include the fear of heights, financial problems, drowning, sickness, death, flying, loneliness, insects, and dogs.

There *are* ways to face fears or overcome them. Sometimes we just need to *do* certain things, even if we're afraid. *Action conquers fear.* You may need to encourage yourself, especially in those last moments before you "rev up your engine."

Even though I'm an experienced public speaker, I still give myself a pep talk every time I speak to a new group. This helps me conquer my fear and focus on others (my audience) rather than myself. I stand in front of a mirror in my hotel room and say, "Yes, Joyce, you can do it. Your message is important and the group needs to hear it!" I stand up straight and do deep breathing exercises. I also consciously relax the muscles in my body and let go of any tension. This can help you to relax and let go of the fear, just as it helps me. With renewed energy and confidence, I go off to do the best I can to help others *become driven by their dreams*, to enable them to live richer, fuller lives.

I belong to the National Speakers Association in the U.S. This fine group, comprised of over 4,000 members, provides a forum for speakers to share speaking techniques, and other secrets for success, with other professional speakers. One of the most important things I have learned from my professional and supportive peers is that many speakers give themselves the same pep talk that I do! We feel the fear and use various ways to overcome it.

You can do the same thing if you feel fear before making a presentation in front of a group or a one-on-one. When you share ideas or your products or services, tell yourself "I can do it. These people need to hear what I have to say." Then relax your shoulders and breathe deeply, ending with "I can do it." Focus out on others rather than inward to yourself—be centered on them and concentrate on helping them.

Too many people give in to their fears, allowing their dread to consume and paralyze them from taking action. Fear really is *false evidence appearing real.* Picture a baby crawling around, exploring their new world. They examine things with curiosity and without fear.

Now step back and consider any situations in your life which usually trigger fear in you. Do your best to understand the situation from the perspective of the other person or people—have empathy for them. Ask yourself, "How would I feel if I were in their shoes?" Then work to change your attitude toward that situation and overcome the fear that held you back. Remember that positive self-talk, breathing deeply, and letting go of any tension in your body can help you tremendously. It's worth the effort!

Worry—the second control buster. Look at the time you may be spending worrying about things that have already happened that you can't change, or things that probably will *never* happen. Worry is mentally reliving a situation that's over and done with, or mentally rehearsing a supposedly potential disaster. It's focusing on a possible worse-case scenario. (Since you get what you focus on, be sure you focus on the positive!) Ask yourself how you want to spend your time: worrying about "what ifs" or living a joyous, happy, fulfilling life? Worry won't extend your life one second or solve any problems. It just depletes your valuable energy and takes your focus off the way you'd like things to be.

Picture yourself looking at a majestic gorge like the Grand Canyon in the U.S. You're contemplating your life, much of which you may have worried away by focusing on the disappointments rather than the good. Say to yourself, "My concerns are so small relative to the magnificence of this beautiful place. It'll still be here, long after my worries are gone. I vow to focus on how fortunate I am in so many ways—to be grateful for the positive things in my life."

Gratitude is essential to happiness. So look for the good in everything—including adversity. Let worry go. Be thankful for what you have and focus only on what you really want—*your dreams and goals.*

In the classic book *How To Stop Worrying And Start Living,* Dale Carnegie quotes American novelist and playwright Booth Tarkington, "...it is in the mind we see and in the mind we live, whether we know it or not." It is essential to banish worry from your life so the precious energy previously used in worrying can then be used to pursue your dream.

My favorite quote about worry is by American author and humorist Mark Twain, "I've had a lot of trouble in my life, most of which never happened!" Think about all the times you wanted to say no to an invitation but you went anyway. Maybe you worried about what you were going to wear, who you would sit with, or who would be there. Afterward, you probably realized how much you enjoyed yourself. In all likelihood, the very things you let gnaw at you never materialized. As French writer, Honoré de Balzac said, many centuries ago, "Our worst misfortunes never happen, and most miseries lie in anticipation."

Do you worry about yesterday and tomorrow? Yesterday has passed and so have any mistakes you have made. We cannot erase a single word we said or act we did. Oftentimes, however, we can apologize or do something else to compensate for our past behavior. We can also forgive ourselves and others and let it go. You can anticipate tomorrow as a great day full of promise and excitement, or a sad day full of regrets and fear. Our attitude is the link to how we experience life. A positive attitude banishes worry!

We have a choice, moment by moment, of how we live today. Think of this moment. Do your best to invest in yourself so you're growing and driving toward your dream. Savor *now* as you enjoy your journey. Stop and smell the flowers along the way. None of us knows what tomorrow will bring, and yesterday is history. Today is all that really matters. Whatever happens to-day—know you can handle it. Make each day a masterpiece!

How many times have you been preoccupied, worrying about things? Did you miss out on what was happening in your present situation because you didn't see the marvelous opportunities right in front of you? Worry does not help tomorrow's challenges, and it ruins today's happiness. British Prime Minister Winston Chur-chill had important advice for us, "Let your advance worrying become advance thinking and planning."

Remember, *we have choices* about our thoughts. We may change pictures on the wall when we've tired of looking at them. How about doing the same thing with your mind? Picture a brilliant red sunset. Notice the sun disappearing into the horizon. Nothing is left except a gorgeous pink sky. Now change your mental picture and see a pitch-black sky with a full moon beaming at you. Visual-ize two cows jumping over the moon. Change your mental picture again. Now see a red fire engine and hear the sirens blaring. Picture yourself behind the wheel wearing the fire chief's hat.

Were you able to imagine those things? You can do the same thing when it comes to worry. Decide right now to let go of worry! It's a habit you can change. You can let go of any habit that isn't serving you and replace it with a new, success-inducing habit. To do so, you need to make the decision that you're *ready* to change your thinking and behavior. *You'll know you're ready to change when the pain of staying the same is greater than your perception of the pain of change.* That tells you it's time to move on to a new experience.

Failure—the third control buster. Failure is only a temporary setback. It is an event, not a person. We can learn our most important lessons of what to do, or not do, through failure. (Those of us who are astute enough to learn from other people's failures are wise indeed!) American automobile manufacturer Henry Ford once said, "Failure is an opportunity to begin again more intelligently."

As a professional speaker I have learned a great deal from failure. I know that every audience will not jump to its feet with applause or run over to me with compliments at the conclusion of each session. They may not laugh at every humorous story, or clap at every magic trick I use to prove a point. Sometimes people don't respond positively. All performers—whether in sports, theater, television, professional speaking, or something else— have those times in their careers when they are disillusioned and feel as though they want to quit. *Learn* from these experiences.

People who quit after failure miss many of life's important lessons. Former NFL and Green Bay Packer football coach Vince Lombardi once said, "It's not whether you get knocked down, it's whether you get up again." The people who win on the road of life are those who consider failure a temporary setback and a normal part of the achievement process. They ask for directions and get right back on the road to achieve their next goal— stronger and wiser *because of* the failure.

Henry Ford also observed, "Obstacles are those frightful things you see when you take your eyes off your goal." As former British Prime Minister Margaret Thatcher once said, "You may have to fight a battle more than once to win it." Winston Churchill stated, "Never, never, never, give in…." And to make your goals and dreams a reality, you need to do the same.

The following is from the rejection notice received when the immensely popular and famous book *The Diary of Anne Frank* was first submitted for publication: "The girl doesn't have a special perception or feeling which would lift that book above the curiosity level." How wrong they turned out to be!

Remember, there are critics everywhere who offer negative comments anytime you choose to step out and do something different. But don't take it personally. What they are saying reflects their own issues, which have nothing to do with what's right for you and your family. If these critics keep focusing on the negative and criticizing you and your actions, you may need to ignore or disassociate yourself from them, at least temporarily.

A man told his father that if he (his dad) continued criticizing his business, he didn't want to see him anymore. Shortly after that, his father wrote him a letter saying how proud he was to be his dad! Remember, *everyone* encounters naysayers on the road of success. Adopt the attitude—*what other people think about what I'm doing is none of my business!*

One workshop participant gave me the following article:

"You've failed many times, although you may not remember. You fell down the first time you tried to walk. You almost drowned the first time you tried to swim, didn't you? Did you hit the ball the first time you swung a bat? Heavy hitters—the ones who hit the most home runs—also strike out a lot. R.H. Macy failed seven times before his department store in New York caught on. An English novelist…once got 753 rejection slips before he published 564 books. Babe Ruth struck out 1,330 times, but he also hit 714 home runs. Don't worry about failure. Worry about the chances you miss when you don't even try."

We dream about the perfect event, the perfect vacation, the perfect relationship, the perfect wedding, and the perfect life. But when we think about it, the stories we retell every year tend to be memories of imperfection—the time Mom dropped the cake, the time Junior broke his arm showing off, and the time Dad missed his surprise party.

The next time you find yourself reeling from something you believe is a terrible failure, remember that, in all likelihood, someday you'll look back and just laugh about it. Then tell yourself, "If someday I'm going to laugh about this anyway, I might as well laugh about it now!" It's amazing how that thinking can help you turn your attitude around.

My mission, as a speaker and trainer, is to plant positive seeds in the minds of my audiences. I am not responsible for the actions they take or don't take—that's up to them. They also get to reap their harvest! They need to decide what changes to make, and what chances to take. My commitment is to coach them to be their personal best. The same is true of you, as one of my readers. I'm here to encourage you and share what I've learned over the years. What you *do* with it is up to you!

Similarly, when you are attending a motivational seminar, keep in mind that speakers can do only so much. They can help you get excited about your dream and encourage you by sharing their story, then suggest what you could do in order to be successful. After that, it's up to you to take the information and drive with it in the direction of your dream.

Years ago, when I was getting ready for one of my first workshops on team building, I gave myself a pep talk. I was prepared to speak to an audience of 50 people. But the minute I began the program I knew I was in trouble. No one made an effort to move after I gave them instructions to find a new partner. Not one person smiled when I told my signature story—one that had always received a positive response before. I was devastated. This was my first flop.

Afterward, I talked to the meeting planner about my dismal results with this group. She told me that the audience had just come from a three-hour cocktail party! Some members wanted to continue partying, while others just wanted to go to sleep. What they didn't want was to hear a program on team building. That certainly explained their lack of response.

I learned some important lessons about my career that day—to take any failures in stride, to do background research, and to look at the agenda of the group prior to any presentation or workshop. I learned to ask what the purpose and goals of the program are. I need to know as much as possible about the audience before I conduct a workshop or make a presentation.

Today, meeting planners and participants express their appreciation of my methods to learn all about their company, association, or organization. That one difficult seminar, years ago, taught me the value of research. To be prepared is key no matter whether you're a professional speaker or make presentations in any business or profession. Do the best you can to get ready, then give it all you've got. But don't wait until you're proficient. Start now and practice, practice, practice. Keep learning from your mistakes and continue to fine-tune as you go. You'll get good at it along the way.

When we are experiencing challenging times in our lives, we need to look really hard for the positives. They may not be obvious but, nonetheless, be assured they are still there! When I came home from that devastating program there were flowers waiting for me. A note, in my husband's handwriting, said, "You may have bombed with that audience, but you are still dynamite with me!"

In the process of going toward our goals we're bound to make mistakes—especially as we develop new skills. If you operate your own business, on a part-time or full-time basis, and you're not as successful as you want to be, consider the words of Lisa M. Amoss, Adjunct Professor of Management at Tulane University: "Entrepreneurs average 3.8 failures before final success. What sets the successful ones apart is their amazing persistence. There are a lot of people out there with good and marketable ideas, but real entrepreneurial types never accept defeat." It takes 15 mistake-filled years for many people to be an "overnight" success! The greatest mistake of all would be to give up.

Adversity—the fourth control buster. Life gives us an opportunity to look for positives in every negative situation. Finding the positive is a real test if we are down and out physically, financially, or emotionally. Yet, as amazing as it may seem, something good always comes from adversity—we just need to recognize it.

Terry, a salesperson and workshop participant, shared with me how getting fired from her first job was the *best* thing that ever happened to her. She always told her prospects, "When you buy our product, I will show you a magic trick." People loved this and she was a high producer in her company. But Terry's boss didn't like her different, yet effective, approach. He told her she didn't fit into the corporate mold and asked her to find employment elsewhere.

At first, Terry was discouraged. She was out of a job and felt like a failure. After some soul-searching, however, she decided to change her focus and teach other salespeople how to use magic when closing a deal. Now she is much more satisfied in her work, makes more money, loves every day of her life, and her blood pressure is normal again. Remember, Terry saw no positives in the situation when she was dismissed, but she was persistent and pursued her dreams and goals.

There are plenty of ways you can focus on the positives and be creative in your response to adversity in your career or business. First ask yourself, "What's good about this situation?" At a minimum, you can learn what *not* to do.

Adversity can teach you a multitude of things, such as: how to communicate more clearly, refining your approach to tasks, upgrading your knowledge and enthusiasm, delegating responsibilities better, and learning to bounce back from disappointments more easily. You could work with your boss, mentor, or leader on this. Just find someone who is open-minded enough to listen to you—someone who has some influence to spearhead the change. They may give you the right insight and ideas that you could use to grow to the next level. And they can also share what's been known to work and not work in your industry.

As a leader, always bear in mind that, just because something failed before, doesn't mean that, with a few modifications, it couldn't work now. After all, things are changing all the time—that's called progress. A good example is the growth of e-commerce and the Internet. Any business that expects to survive and thrive needs to embrace the new technology and incorporate it into their operations.

Whenever you have a good idea, share it. And during the process, always respect others' feelings, ideas, and policies. Don't expect things to change overnight. Just be patient and keep going.

If you are a business owner associated with a group of other people, perhaps where there's a success system already in place, check with your leadership before you do anything that may contradict that system. After all, your idea may have already been used and found not to work. There's no use in repeating the mistake.

At any rate, be persistent! You may find your idea is new and that your creativity leads to a significant change for the better, both for yourself and others. So when you have a good idea, keep persevering until someone who can help you takes you seriously!

A life-changing event for me began when I was hired to speak in the Cayman Islands to a group of record store managers from the U.S. My son, Ron, accompanied me to assist with the program. We became acquainted with this extraordinary group of people before the presentation, and enjoyed the blue sky and perfect weather of the islands.

Suddenly, we learned a hurricane was fast approaching. The hotel personnel instructed us to quickly gather our valuables and board the buses which would take us to hurricane shelters. The constable even asked us to sign papers denoting next of kin! He said the island was flat and the waves could drown us if the winds reached the expected 200 miles per hour.

I allowed fear to overwhelm me and began to panic. I regretted bringing my son along, believing it may have been a mistake. But Ron strongly and lovingly encouraged me to stop worrying, because things could turn out alright after all. Ron jolted me out of my fear with his calm reassurance.

We heard the howling winds and the sounds of uprooted trees crashing to the ground. The roof of another hurricane shelter caved in and 200 more people joined us in our already crowded quarters. We heard the death count from the storm in Jamaica on the radio.

People were concerned about their loved ones on other islands. Some were screaming—others were out of control. Ron and I started talking to total strangers about how we would change our lives if we survived. Fortunately, the eye of the hurricane missed us by 20 miles.

This near tragedy taught me a great deal about myself and my life—more than I had ever understood before the hurricane.

First, we all need to be flexible, like the reed in Aesop's fable. We never know when hurricanes or other challenges will come into our lives.

Second, it doesn't matter who we are or where we come from, we all have inner resources that make us strong. The magic is not in how we deal with normal everyday situations, but in how we deal with the daily stresses in our lives. We need to know how to deal effectively with adversity in order to become successful. Then we can appreciate our success and those who helped us get there, and not to take either for granted.

Third, when we face death, we value life even more. Every single day becomes more precious. We learn to stay away from people who complain and moan about trivial things, yet refuse to do something about their circumstances. Such people only bog us down.

Fourth, we are reminded of the importance of our value system as I was—my family comes before my career!

My priorities were in the wrong order before Hurricane Gilbert blew into my life. I was putting more energy into my career than my family. I was on a treadmill and didn't even realize it. Now I see how my family helps to keep me going. When I put them first, they put me first by encouraging me to pursue my speaking. They are my coaches, cheering me on when I get an exciting speaking engagement, and gently kicking me in the seat of my pants when I need it. I learned never to take them for granted.

You may not face death or hurricanes every day but you do face obstacles. Ask yourself, "How would I react if a storm hit me?" "How much do I appreciate what I have now?" "Do I value my loved ones, my health, my job or business?" As Will Rogers once said, "Nothing makes a person more broad-minded like adversity."

People Pleasing—the fifth control buster. Many of us have been taught, since childhood, to be passive—to obey our elders—our parents, our teachers, and others who are in charge of our environment and where we live. We were taught to do what these people told us to do, without questions. As children, of course, we weren't ready to make certain decisions. So this guidance served as a protective mechanism to compensate for our youthful exuberance and inexperience.

The most fortunate of us were encouraged, little by little, to assume more and more responsibility for making choices as well as expressing our needs and wants. First, we were allowed to choose what clothes we were going to wear that day. Or perhaps we were permitted to decide what kind of ice cream we'd like at the local soda shop. Ideally, the decisions we were allowed to make were of more and more importance as we grew into adulthood.

Some of our parents were better at encouraging us to think for ourselves. Others, though, maintained strict control over what their children did. They didn't help us develop the ability to share honestly what we needed and wanted, especially if what we said was contradictory to their idea of how things should be done. We may not have been taught to make wise choices and act on our own. Those parents believed the best approach was to be protective and controlling of us. Whatever our parents did, however, they were doing the best they could with their level of understanding at the time.

As we grew up, some of us became passive. We may have adopted "people pleasing" ways in an effort to be accepted, rather than responding thoughtfully and honestly, expressing our true needs and wants. We may *try* to figure out what others want, with or without asking them, and do what we *believe* they want—simply to avoid rejection. In fact, some people are so into the habit of doing this that they don't even realize it.

Being an employee means having certain responsibilities and doing the best job possible—that's a given. But some people are constantly in a people pleasing mode around their boss and everyone else at work. No matter what demands are put on them, they accommodate everyone in an attempt to win their favor.

As time passes, people pleasers develop a growing discontent because they rarely get what they want. They feel abused and taken advantage of. They're constantly "stuffing down" their feelings and ideas. They usually blame others and believe they're a victim. They may become robotic and passive, afraid to speak up. As their unhappiness increases, they lash out at others for being selfish. They don't realize they may be fooling themselves by thinking blind compliance is what others expect and want of them.

The people pleaser may smile on the outside, as a mask for their mounting dissatisfaction, and growl on the inside. Such people are seriously prone to burnout. After all, it takes a lot of energy to accommodate others, especially when it's a win-lose situation, and they're the ones losing. They've given up control and have let themselves be at the mercy of others. Notice I said "let" themselves—no one is forcing them to live like this. The best thing they can do is to simply be themselves.

The people pleaser can be such a chameleon—changeable depending on what they believe someone else wants them to be—that no one knows *what* they want! Ironically, if they would say what they want, they'd probably get it. The strain people pleasers put on themselves is unnecessary.

In a business situation, the people pleaser may, blindly and unthinkingly, follow the dictates of the boss. But many employers and leaders like hearing from their people. For instance, considerable cost savings could be realized with a new approach. The leader may accept or reject the idea, ask for more information, or be inspired to come up with an even better suggestion because of what was shared!

In any case, it's always the leader's right to make the final decision. So if you really want your ideas to be taken seriously, be a leader!

Respecting and considering your employees' and business associates' wants, needs, and feelings can be time intensive. But the long-term payoffs can be considerable—like more harmonious, happy relationships. And when it comes to encouraging and nurturing mutual respect, it's always more effective coming from the leader.

If people are shut down from communicating, they may find that being agreeable is their only choice—in an effort to please the leader. This attitude hastens burnout as it affects the morale of the people and the quality and quantity of their work. As a result, some may choose to leave the organization.

Unfortunately, if the leader doesn't learn flexibility and open-mindedness in listening to their people, it's likely they'll repeat the same behavior with others, and get similar results.

People pleasing habits can show up in all areas of our lives. Some of us are so accustomed to shutting down and reacting passively to our environment that we need to make a special effort to realize our own feelings, wants, and needs! We may be so used to putting up with things we don't like that we need to stop and take inventory of who we are and what we *really, really,* want.

This involves uncovering what's honestly in our hearts and minds and sharing that courageously and persistently. We may get responses like "I didn't know you wanted that—we could have easily done it." "A new chair for your office isn't in the budget, but I'll see what I can do." "I'm really sorry, but we can't accommodate your request." At this point we may decide to talk to someone with more power, if we seriously want what we asked for.

Remember this—*no one's going to be committed to your agenda more than you.* Everyone else has their own concerns—yours is not likely to be at the top of anyone else's list. So, as the cliché goes, "The squeaky wheel gets the grease." Persevere with what's important to you.

To be your happiest, create win-win situations. If a decision is clearly win-lose and you're on the "losing end of the stick," it's up to *you* to take action. You can ask for help, but don't expect anyone else to overcome your challenge for you. It's yours to *grow through.* And when victory comes, it will be even sweeter. Make it a fun game.

People pleasers often blame others for their difficulties. We all need to determine how our behavior contributed to the situation. You might be highly respected and admired by many, yet have trouble saying no when someone asks you to do something you don't want to do.

If you're truly torn between choices, you could say, "I'll think about it and let you know." Then you could search your heart and mind for what you really want to do. After all, it's *your* life.

People can take unfair advantage of us, *but only if we let them.* How are others to know what we want, especially if we don't tell them? Anyone caught up in people pleasing needs to practice expressing their thoughts and feelings in a kind, yet firm way. Expecting others to know what we want, is likely to result in disappointments. We need to be proactive—*be the initiator of action.*

For example, you may have a job where you're required to work on certain weekends. Suppose a co-worker friend asks you to work for him on one of your off weekends when you already have family plans. Do you automatically say yes in an effort to please your friend and then suffer the consequences at home? Or do you thoughtfully respond that you already have a family commitment on that weekend and therefore won't be available to work, and suggest he ask someone else?

It's okay to please people as long as you're not selling yourself short. Just be aware of what you may be sacrificing if you say yes, and be sure you're okay with that. If you're on the losing end of too many interactions, and frustrated that you rarely get what you want, then it's time for you to assert yourself.

The short-term pain avoidance of habitually complying with others' wishes can have long-term negative consequences to your health and well-being. Ignoring your own wants and needs can lead to bursts of anger that seem to come out of nowhere. This is often the result of the built-up resentment that comes from constantly deferring to others' desires, at the expense of your own heartfelt wishes.

Not everyone is going to agree with you, no matter what you do. Just do your best to create win-win situations and let other people's opinions be their own business. We all need to do the right thing, considering our responsibilities. Just gather your nerve and do it! Be confident it'll all work out in the end.

Eliminate any purely passive habits you may have by thinking before you respond. Be as real as you can. Risk having your ideas rejected. If you feel a restraining tug inside you, step back and re-think what you really want.

Ask yourself if what you're about to do supports you in achieving your goals. If it doesn't, what alternatives do you have? Ask questions. And above all—*ask for what you want.* Don't assume anything. Respond in a friendly way, yet firmly and with fairness, when you need to say no. Say, "I appreciate your asking me. I already have a commitment that day."

All five control busters—fear, worry, failure, adversity, and people pleasing—can be met and conquered. Realize how strong you really are. Change your mental channels whenever fear and worry come into your mind. Ask yourself, "What's the worst thing that could happen in this situation?" and accept it. See failures as learning experiences and stepping stones to success. Look within and you'll find inner strength whenever adversity strikes. Respond compassionately and honestly when you're tempted to fall into the people-pleasing mode. Don't let anything stop you from going *full speed ahead!*

At the end of each day stop and look at what went *right*. If you were told you'd have only six months to live, what would you do differently today? Roman philosopher Marcus Aurelius wrote, "Execute every day of life as though it were your last." Live each day fully and face and overcome your challenges courageously. You *can* make your dreams come true—one day at a time.

Now Implement the *Full Speed Ahead* Action Plan...

Determine whether you are prone to burnout by taking a few moments now to respond to these questions, checking either yes or no.

	Yes	No
1. Do you consider yourself a perfectionist?	___	___
2. Do you find it difficult to say no?	___	___
3. Do you frequently skip meals because you are too busy to eat?	___	___
4. Do you never have enough time to do what you want?	___	___

	Yes	No
5. Do you find it difficult to delegate authority?	____	____
6. Do you feel guilty about your inability to do everything?	____	____
7. Do you handle chores and situations as they arise rather than planning ahead?	____	____
8. Do you rarely relax, exercise, have fun, dreambuild, or do something else beneficial for yourself?	____	____
9. Do you feel you have no control over your situation?	____	____
10. Are you always catering to the needs of others, while ignoring your own?	____	____

Now check your score. Give yourself 10 points for every yes answer:

0-20	Under control
30-40	Some control buster characteristics
50-60	More control buster characteristics
70-100	Mostly control buster characteristics

The higher your score, the more likely you're burning yourself out by being fearful, worried, concerned about failure, resisting adversity, and being passive—running around, trying to please others, and putting out "fires." You may often be dealing with challenges that could have been prevented and that you can avoid in the future.

The more control you gain over how you cope with challenges, the more energy you'll have to drive *full speed ahead* to your dream. Remember, your friends don't pay your bills. It's up to you to take charge of any situation you may be allowing to detour you from achieving your dream. You're in the driver's seat—it's up to you! Other people have overcome the control busters and you can too!

Write down the new ideas you have learned in this chapter. Make a copy of this plan and place it in a prominent location in your home or office. Make sure you do all of the things you have made note of. Here are a couple of examples to get you started.

1. Do something that'll bring you closer to your dream, such as test driving your fantasy car and touring your dream neighborhood.
2. Do something kind for yourself such as hiring a babysitter and go out on a date with your spouse.

Top performers are people who realize they need to take care of themselves first, mentally and physically. They are in control of their own lives, their thinking and behavior, even during stressful times. They take their lives seriously and themselves lightly. How do you take care of your own needs during stressful times?

Here are three examples to get you started. Write down a few more on a sheet of paper and put it in a prominent location in your home or office.

1. Start taking vitamins and supplements if you're not eating properly and talk to a nutritionist.
2. Take a brisk 20 minute walk 3-5 times a week with your family.
3. Take a half hour nap if you were up late the night before.

Chapter 3

Fill Up Your Tank with High-Octane Humor!

*"Humor is an affirmation of your dignity. It shows you are
bigger than all your challenges."*
Anonymous

Laughter Is the Best Medicine

Each day more and more people understand the value of humor in improving their lives. As a result, we are buying more personal development books and tapes than ever before. Many people want to know:

- ◆ How can I lighten up?
- ◆ How do I deal with the pressures of today's stressful world?
- ◆ How can I feel more relaxed at home?
- ◆ How can I bring excitement back into my personal relationships?
- ◆ How can I make my job or business more fun and enjoyable?
- ◆ How can I become closer to my family members?

In this chapter, you will learn how to add more fun to your daily life and bring out the humor that already exists.

You may be saying, "I'm not a funny person. I can't tell jokes. My life is full of pressure and nothing enjoyable or funny ever happens to me." However, you *do* have the ability to have more positive experiences, at home, on your job, in your business, and virtually any place you are. The answers lie within you.

The seven main themes in this chapter are:

1. The importance of humor.
2. The difference between childlike and childish behavior.
3. How to have fun.
4. How to take yourself lightly and your life seriously.
5. How to develop a sense of joy in your life.
6. How corporations, government agencies, and organizations use humor to increase productivity.
7. Exciting ideas to get you started.

I ask my workshop participants to brainstorm this question: "How can you guarantee yourself a life that is totally serious and dull?" At first they look confused, then they begin to have fun with the question. They answer:

♦ Don't play with your children.
♦ Don't read the comics.
♦ Don't go after your dreams
♦ Concentrate on the sad times in life.
♦ Never cheer up a person who needs encouragement.
♦ Take yourself very seriously and condemn yourself when you make a mistake.
♦ Don't laugh for fear someone may think you are silly and childish.
♦ Don't smile because smiles give you wrinkles.

The greeting card industry is extremely successful with its comical cards. Humor in advertising is refreshing, provides stress relief, and sells more products and services. People need escape from the pressure of constant demands—especially in the more high-paced areas of the world.

It's key to associate with positive-thinking people and have some fun. We want and need to laugh; it's healthy. Of course, humor is not for anyone who wants to stay in their negative-thinking rut. It's only for people who want to upgrade their attitude, feel happy, encourage others, feel more alive, and enjoy life!

Many people aren't very good at telling jokes. Those who are good joke tellers have lucrative careers—thanks to good material, expert timing, delivery, pizzazz, courage, determination, and talent. We may groan when our friends tell a joke and stumble over the punch line. While you may not necessarily be funny, just do your best at being fun to be with.

Some people are always joking, trying too hard to be liked, and attempting to hide their lack of confidence behind a facade of humor. You never really get to know such people. So their relationships tend to be superficial. Endeavor to be as genuine as possible, rather than just using humor to hide behind.

Consider the people you like to be around. Are they funny, always cracking jokes, or do they find the humor in daily events? Are they fun to be with? Are you fun to be with?

By now, you may be wondering how this book can help you lighten up. Read on.

"Someday I will laugh at this" is a statement most everyone makes at least once in their life. But why wait for someday? As mentioned earlier, if you are going to look back on something years later and laugh, why wait? Laugh now!

People say, "I will have fun. But not now, I'm much too busy. I'll have fun on vacation or on my day off." Don't postpone joy and laughter. You never know what tomorrow will bring, or even if it will come. How sad it is to see people waste their precious today.

Some of my favorite quotes are:

- ◆ "The really happy person is one who can enjoy the scenery on a detour."—Anonymous
- ◆ Comedian George Burns quipped, "If I get big laughs, I'm a comedian. If I get little laughs, I'm a humorist. If I get no laughs, I'm a singer."
- ◆ Greek philosopher Plato stated, "Life should be lived as a play."

♦ "Happiness consists of living each day as if it were the first day of your honeymoon and the last day of your vacation."—Anonymous

Humor Can Increase Productivity

People are often surprised to learn that as they incorporate humor into their lives, it helps them develop a new set of skills and a fresh outlook on life. They find that, as a result, all areas of their lives are positively affected. Here are five key reasons why humor is so important:

1. Humor can increase learning and productivity—personally and professionally.
2. Laughter is great for your well-being.
3. You can weather a challenging situation more easily when you laugh—it helps you release stress.
4. Humor helps you not only survive but thrive in the face of change.
5. Laughter helps you stay young at heart.

During challenging times, humor relieves tension and keeps us flexible and fluid—not rigid and breakable. As water brings life to any environment, humor nurtures your quality of life. It helps you to have a positive attitude regardless of what's happening. Humor makes it seem more worth the effort to overcome the obstacles on the road to your dream.

Successful corporations are discovering that people work more effectively and productively when humor is part of their workday. When you have fun with your job or business, you'll attract more positive-thinking people to associate with. Nobody wants a dull, boring occupation! People want to have fun—to enjoy what they do and who they're with. As the saying goes, *"We don't stop playing because we get old. We get old because we stop playing."*

Research shows that when people play more enthusiastically they stay healthier. The French physician Voltaire wrote in 1770, "The art of medicine consists of amusing the patient while nature cures the disease." English satirist Jonathan Swift wrote, "The best doctors in the world are Dr. Diet, Dr. Quiet, and Dr. Merryman."

Humor is serious business! It helps us relax, be flexible, have a positive attitude, and remain creative while under pressure. Brainstorming sessions tumble along like white water and new ideas pour out when people laugh. Have fun at your next get-together with your business associates. Lightness helps you move along and enjoy the journey.

Humor helps us thrive in the midst of constant change. Some people allow themselves to be defeated, not by the change itself but, by their own rigidity. A young father told his son, "Things were so difficult when I was your age. I actually had to get up off the couch and walk across the room to change the TV channels!"

Think about the changes in your life since you were a child. It's likely to be quite amazing. Did you ever notice that when you stepped outside of yourself and laughed at the challenges along the way, you were able to deal with them much more easily?

A Good Sense of Humor Will Help with a Major Challenge

The value of humor is best reflected in the midst of big challenges. You'll find that, through humor, you're better able to overcome the large obstacles and weather storms with only short-term, if any, detours. Then you can breeze through the minor everyday challenges—you'll have developed a great solution-oriented, fun-loving attitude. Having a sense of humor as you passionately pursue your dream helps make the trip smoother and quicker.

When I was in graduate school, I thought it was inappropriate when a professor had comedians come in to speak at a class on death and dying. Mothers and fathers of deceased children also spoke and shared their grieving process with us. I was surprised when the parents related how humor helped them get through their pain.

After the death of my wonderful father, Joseph, I also learned how humor could help me cope through the grieving process. Instead of concentrating on his last few months in a hospital bed, I shifted my focus. I reminded myself of all the happy times I had with him. I smile when I recall his reaction to my teenage antics.

To those who have teenagers, remember that the events that drive you crazy now will turn into funny stories that make you laugh in the future. So why not laugh now?

I have come to realize the necessity of humor in my training sessions also. When I discuss serious subjects, I include an element of fun to add lightness—it helps keep the audience positive. A few years ago I added magical illusions to my workshops. People tell me they enjoy the magic and ask for more. They love it because it's a high-energy experience and injects the element of fun into each session. The tricks and levity reinforce a rule I live by—take yourself lightly and your life seriously. Again, have fun with your job or business. Be kind to yourself and learn from and laugh about the challenges. In most cases, a year (or maybe even a day) from now you'll have forgotten them. So enjoy each day!

I remember an incident that happened when my son, Ron, was moving from our home to his first apartment. He decided to be creative and throw something (rather than carry it) from the upstairs loft down to the first floor. In the process, he destroyed my favorite piece of crystal. He felt awful when he heard the glass crash to the floor. I saw the look of panic on his face.

My first inclination was to yell and scream and to tell him that his actions were reckless and irresponsible. Instead, I exerted self-control and mustered up as much of a humorous attitude as I could and said, "Crystal can be replaced. It is more important for you to never repeat that brilliant move again!" As a humor and self-esteem coach I had to remind myself to practice what I preach!

My response fit with my value system. How would it have helped matters if I had criticized him and negatively affected his self-esteem? Ron laughs today at how my words sounded so right and so nonjudgmental—while my clenched jaw showed him that I was really upset.

I asked myself how important this broken glass would be two years from now versus his self-esteem. He thanks me today. Ron is married now and I am confident that he, as a father, will do his best to preserve and enhance his children's self-esteem. And I'm positive he'll always regard challenging situations as humorously as he can.

As American actress Ethel Barrymore noted, "You grow up the day you have your first real laugh—at yourself." Sir Winston Churchill was once asked, "Doesn't it thrill you to know that every time you make a speech the hall is overflowing?" He responded, "It is quite flattering. But whenever I feel that way I always remember that if instead of making a political speech I was being hanged, the crowd would be twice as big!"

Did you know that every U.S. president since Franklin D. Roosevelt has had a gag writer on his team? President Harry Truman mused, "Any man who has had the job I've had and didn't possess a sense of humor wouldn't still be here."

Laugh at Yourself and Build Better Relationships

Comedian Jimmy Durante once said, "It dawned on me that as long as I could laugh I was safe from the world; and I have learned since that laughter keeps me safe from myself, too. All of us have schnozes (noses) that are ridiculous in one way or another, if not on our faces, then in our characters, minds, or habits. When we admit our schnozes, instead of defending them, we begin to laugh, and the world laughs with us."

"Everything is funny as long as it is happening to someone else," Will Rogers observed. *People who can laugh at themselves can relate better to others by showing their vulnerabilities.* This is part of being genuine. If you want to make people laugh, just poke fun at yourself but never at anyone else. I notice that people give me more eye contact when I tell of my own blunders. We *love* to hear others share stories about their mistakes. It helps us accept and laugh about our own goof-ups!

Smiling and laughter are key ingredients to a well-rounded life. It takes less energy to smile—only 17 of your muscles! However, you use 43 muscles to frown. One of my favorite sayings is, "Keep smiling. It makes people wonder what you've been up to!" This is true of people who have a positive attitude because they're focusing on and driving toward their dream. They have a sparkle in their eyes and a bounce in their step.

The *American Heritage Dictionary Of The English Language* defines laughing like this—"To express certain emotions, especially mirth, delight, or derision, by a series of spontaneous, usually unarticulated sounds often accompanied by corresponding facial and bodily movements."

Endorphins Are Released by Laughter, Reaching Goals, and Making Dreams Come True!

Are you familiar with endorphins—chemicals that are produced in the brain? Their structure almost matches synthetic morphine and, as a result, they can deliver pain relief similar to certain medications. They elevate the "inner uppers," a phrase coined by Dr. Dale Anderson, that raise our spirits and lift our moods.

Thirty-seven endorphins are released by laughing, satisfying relationships, setting and reaching goals, being with groups of positive-thinking people, exercising regularly, and soaking up nature. Picture the last time you had a really good belly laugh. Was it a natural high? If so, your endorphins were flowing. And didn't you feel great the last time you accomplished a goal or made a dream come true? Wow!

Here are some great expressions on laughter. A Yiddish proverb states, "What soap is to the body, laughter is to the soul." As comedian Milton Berle once said, "Laughter is an instant vacation." Mark Twain remarked, "The human race has only one really effective weapon, and that is laughter." Scottish novelist Sir James Barrie noted, "Those who bring sunshine to the lives of others cannot keep it from themselves." Author Norman Cousins reported, "Laughter is a form of internal jogging. Ten minutes of genuine belly laughter has an anesthetic effect and will give me at least two hours of pain-free sleep." Comedian Victor Borge quipped, "Laughter is the shortest distance between two people." And last of all—the definition of a belly laugh—a mirthquake!

What's the Difference Between Childish and Childlike Behavior?

Some people have a problem distinguishing between childish and childlike behavior. Childishness is undesirable, and childlikeness is admirable. People with childish qualities often display selfish, immature, and even infantile behavior like blaming, whining, pouting, and throwing tantrums. They exhibit failure rather than success-inducing behaviors. On the other hand, people who have childlike qualities have a sense of innocence and are curious, open, spontaneous, flexible, optimistic, creative, playful, trusting, and joyful.

When my workshop participants divide into groups to discuss ideas, they often display delightful childlike behavior. The noise level increases when I ask them to rediscover and talk about their favorite childhood games and songs. It is refreshing to hear their joyous laughter. Every time people act childlike in a workshop something positive comes from the experience. Think about the fun you had with your favorite game, playmate, or toys when you were a child. You're starting to smile...aren't you?

Some adults with unhappy, negative-thinking, close-minded attitudes think people who laugh aren't very intelligent and don't take life seriously. Perhaps they're abiding by the old adage— misery loves company. It's unfortunate they don't see the importance of humor in our lives. American poet Robert Frost wrote, "Forgive my nonsense as I also forgive the nonsense of those who think they talk sense."

To become childlike some people need to loosen up and overcome the messages from their past like, "Wipe that smile off your face!" or "Wait until *you* have children!" Are you one of those people? Be assured that it's okay to have fun—in fact, it's highly recommended!

Again, people need to take themselves lightly and their world seriously. For example, laugh at the mistakes you make and the various situations you encounter as you build your career or business. Have fun with it! Laugh, learn, and keep on going—*full speed ahead.* The old English word for silly means to be happy or prosperous. With these qualities in mind, the value of childlike, innocent behavior becomes even more apparent, doesn't it?

People Learn More When They're Having Fun

When the people in my audiences see me having a good time, they're more likely to be enjoying the experience too. Fun is contagious. I come by this childlike quality honestly. My mother, Sara, is the kind of person others love to be around. She has a positive outlook, an engaging smile, and is fun to be with. My mother is living proof of one of my favorite expressions, "We are only young once, but with humor, we can be youthful forever."

Charlie "Tremendous" Jones and Bob Phillips, in their book *Wit & Wisdom,* share some high-octane humor:

"When someone says, 'I do not wish to appear critical,' it means he (or she) is going to let you have it."

"...that when someone says, 'It's only money,' it's usually your money he's talking about."

"My husband didn't leave me a bit of insurance."
"Then where did you get the gorgeous diamond ring?"
"Well, he left $1,000 for his casket and $5,000 for a stone. This is the stone."

If you laughed at these humorous comments about life, you're on your way to filling up with high-octane humor! When you're able to laugh at yourself and your challenges, you'll be more likely to attract positive-thinking, fun-loving people into your life.

Go ahead and write some appropriate jokes on a 3"×5" card. Keep it with you and share the jokes with others. You don't have to be great at telling jokes—it doesn't matter. Just have fun with it. Brighten their day and yours, too! Be a positive-thinking, lighthearted example for others. You can do it!

Illusionist David Copperfield ends his incredible show with this message, "Never give up your childlike sense of wonder and joy. Nothing is as important as keeping the magic alive. So smile often, laugh, and have a fun-loving spirit of adventure as you travel the road of success."

Now Implement the *Full Speed Ahead* Action Plan...

Plan something fun every day for a month; just telling a joke counts! Get together with someone, for example an employee or business associate you're mentoring, and order an ice cream cone.

Look at a vehicle you've been dreaming of owning and take a test drive. Draw a smiley face with soap on your spouse's bathroom mirror. Write on their napkin, "You are loved." Keep a record of your experiences either in your day planner or use the Fun Activities chart. Notice the positive effects on your life and relationships.

	Week 1	Week 2	Week 3	Week 4
Sun				
Mon				
Tues				
Wed				
Thurs				
Fri				
Sat				

When you discover new ideas for having fun, or ways of performing a task better, write them down. And be sure you do all of the things you have made note of.

If your new idea is related to building your career or business, check with your mentor. Someone may have tried it before and failed. Or it may be a really great idea that could make a positive difference, perhaps, organization-wide!

Top performers are people who take responsibility for their own morale. People who win focus on the positive rather than letting negativity drain away their energy. They are solution-oriented and rise above their circumstances, injecting humor whenever they can. They realize they are coaches for themselves and others—that their example is the best and most powerful teacher. How they act and what they say, personally and professionally, sets the tone for those around them. A lighthearted, yet responsible, attitude can go a long way in making your life and the lives of others more pleasant!

What can you do today to increase your own morale and boost your attitude? Listen to a positive and uplifting tape. Read a personal development book. Go to a motivational/educational seminar. Give yourself a pep talk. Call someone you respect and ask for support. Write down everything you're grateful for. Go dreambuilding— drive your favorite car, see your dream house, or ask for a vacation day off from work.

What is your attitude adjustment plan? Write it down now and place a copy of it in a prominent location in your home or office. Remember—*the choices you make on a daily basis affect what you will be, do, or have in the tomorrows of your life.*

Chapter 4

Having Fun—Tune Up Your "Funny Bone"

"Whatever you do, keep it fun. People like to be around people who are having fun."
Anonymous

Learning to Have Fun Again

Now that you are probably feeling reassured that it's okay to act childlike at times, let's discover more about how to have fun. Workshop participants sometimes say to me, "I like this workshop and the way it makes me feel. But you don't know me, my family, or my job. There is never anything funny happening to me. Tell me how I can put fun into my everyday life."

Even those of you who share these feelings can learn, with practice, to have fun! You can experience fun and humor. Like unrealized potential, they can be found nearly everywhere; we just need to look for them! As American writer Henry Mencken once observed, "Human life is basically a comedy.... Happiness probably consists largely in the capacity to detect and relish the humor in life."

Start with this exercise. Look around you for red items. You'll see red in clothes, food, rugs, furniture, buildings, signs, nature, hair, cosmetics, toys, and other things. The same principle applies when we search for humor and fun. It may take time; but once you are attuned to looking for humor, you will easily find it.

Every time I perform a magical illusion to make a point in one of my workshops, something funny happens! One time I was doing a trick that required a volunteer assistant from the audience. While my back was turned, she was to choose one of three different colored cards, which were displayed so the audience could see them. Through a series of questions I was going to be able to identify which color they selected. I asked the volunteer to picture herself helping a friend select a color for a new car. I then asked the volunteer what color the friend chose.

The assistant's answer was supposed to end the illusion. But instead, the volunteer started giving a long speech on how she couldn't make a decision for a friend because that would not teach self-responsibility! She went on and on with her explanation. The other participants started laughing, thinking the volunteer was part of the magic trick! I am definitely more careful when selecting an assistant now. But if the illusion does not work out as anticipated, I can always find humor in some aspect of the experience.

As writer Nathaniel Hawthorne once said, "Happiness is a butterfly, which, when pursued, is always just beyond your grasp. But if you sit down quietly, it may settle on you." Helen Keller, American memorist and lecturer, who learned to speak even though she was born deaf and blind, said the following, which makes a lot of sense to me: "When one door of happiness closes, another opens, but often we look so long at the closed door that we don't see the one that has been opened for us."

Inject Humor into Your Life Daily

People can inject humor into their daily lives in countless ways. A doctor in New York had a 22-year-old son and a 26-year-old daughter. He set up his answering machine message to respond to these grown children. He taped a message somewhat similar to the following:

"If you just had a high-volume discussion with your boyfriend or girlfriend and need to talk about it, press one. If you require financial assistance, press two. If you believe you are being treated unfairly at work or school, and wish to express your anger to an understanding family member, press three. If your car or household appliances need immediate repair or replacement, press four. If you are telephoning to inquire about our well-being or to pass a few moments of pleasant topical conversation, please check the number you intended to dial!"

Go ahead and start smiling—we've got some great new jokes to share with you!

A friend's 12-year-old son brought home 4 Ds and 3 Fs on his report card. The boy asked his father, "What do you think my problem is, heredity or environment?"

The following is from the book *Humor Is Tremendous* by Charlie "Tremendous" Jones and Bob Phillips: "Sign on office bulletin board: In case of fire, don't panic. Simply flee the building with the same reckless abandon that occurs each day at quitting time." Their description of the boss is "He's (or she's) the one who watches the clock during the office break."

One day a mother was visiting her son in the hospital. He had just lost his father (her husband), whom they both loved dearly, in a train shooting. He was seriously injured himself—brain damaged and paralyzed. Not surprisingly, his mother noticed that he needed encouragement. So she gave him a pep talk about courage and perseverance.

The son looked at his mom and said, to her surprise, "I want to be handicapped." "Why?" she asked, as calmly as she could. The son looked squarely at his mother and, with a twinkle in his eye, replied, "Better parking!" At that moment she knew he was still a fighter and that everything would be fine. Even though his circumstances were hardly ideal, her son had maintained his sense of humor. The fact is our circumstances, whatever they may be, can be a catalyst to lighten up. Focus on the positive and laugh at life's challenges. As soon as tomorrow, you may not even think about what happened today. And if you do, you can laugh about it because it's over.

Find Humor in Travel Hassles

Most anyone who has flown on an airplane has a funny story about a late arrival, lost luggage, or food they didn't like. Instead of concentrating on what didn't go as expected on your trip, start looking for the funny episodes and what went well. For example, your airplane may have arrived behind schedule at your first layover. Think of all the exercise you got as you sprinted through the airport to get on your next plane!

It's easier to laugh at any situation once you've resolved it. Yet, seeing the absurdity while you're in the middle of it, helps you maintain a calm composure in the process of overcoming the challenge. You overcome it, rather than allowing it to overcome you!

One of my flights was delayed for over an hour. A lot of the passengers were in and out of their seats and many were grumbling. As takeoff time approached, the pilot said, "Ladies and gentlemen, will you please clear the aisles and take your seats so I can see out of the rear view mirror!" As the plane taxied onto the runway, he made a few more humorous remarks. This eased the tension, helped the passengers relax, and put them in a better mood.

Another pilot explained why the airplane was in a holding pattern. "We're experiencing a slight delay, but it is nothing to worry about. They're turning the airport around, and we're going to wait up here until they get it just right for us." The passengers smiled and relaxed.

Pretend it's a hot day and you are taking a walk in your neighborhood. You see a house with a yard sale sign posted in the front yard. (People in the U.S. post this sign when they want to sell things they don't want anymore.) You stop and ask your neighbor, who is out weeding the flower garden, "How much is it?" Looking perplexed, she says, "How much is what?" You respond, "The yard. You have a sign saying you're selling it!" They chuckle.

Picture yourself in the grocery store. You spot a product labeled "fat free." Ask the clerk who's stocking the shelves, "Do you know what 'fat free' means?" They may give you a blank look like they have no idea. So jump in and offer, "There's no charge for the fat!" See if this brings a smile to their face.

A publisher recently asked one of his authors how he enjoyed writing a magazine column he had just acquired. The author laughed and responded, "I sort of feel like the window washer who fell off his scaffolding at the 54th floor. As he whizzed by the 21st floor he shouted, "So far, so good!"

These little stories show us that we can find humor in almost every situation, almost anywhere. We can choose to concentrate on the negatives and walk around with a furrowed brow. Or we can look past them and find the things that are comical in our lives. We can brighten our own days and those of others as we share funny stories. Have you ever heard the comment, "Truth is stranger than fiction"? Well, it can also be said that "Truth is funnier than fiction"!

What Kind of Example Are You Setting?

Another idea to consider is the positive example you are setting by responding to situations in a more thoughtful, fun way. Reacting angrily, and letting yourself be immobilized by frustration, doesn't serve you or anyone else. And it certainly doesn't help you deal with the situation at hand. It just gets you upset and frazzled. Sometimes the only thing you can control in a situation is your attitude. And when you do, look for the good, no matter what happens.

As you build your business or profession, you may not be aware that some people may be looking to you as a role model. This is especially true if you are in a leadership capacity in your community, profession, or in your own business. The fact is, no matter what our roles are, we teach by example. This is true whether it's employees, business associates, children, friends, or other adults outside of your immediate circle observing and taking cues from your behavior. You do affect others—probably more than you realize. So let's take positive advantage of that reality and affect them in a way that enhances your life and theirs. How about it?

Lighten Up and Thrive

Now that we've discussed where to find humor, let's concentrate on learning how to lighten up, which most people want and need to learn. Yes, how we live our lives is a serious responsibility. Yes, business can certainly be challenging. And, yes, we can create a lot of pressure for ourselves. For all these reasons we need to take our lives seriously and ourselves lightly. Abraham Lincoln remarked, "Most folks are about as happy as they make up their minds to be."

C.W. Metcalf, known as the humor-coach, tells a story about Chuck, a brave little boy who was dying. Chuck said, "I want you to give this list to my mom and dad after I die. It's a list of all the fun we had and all the times we laughed. Like the time Mom, Dad, Chrissie, Linda, and I dressed like those guys in an old Fruit of the Loom™ underwear commercial.

"Dad was driving us to a costume party when the police stopped our car for speeding. Dad was dressed like a bunch of grapes and I was an apple, and the others were different things like bananas and other fruits. When the policewoman came up to the car, she looked in and started laughing really hard. I mean, she could hardly stand up. We all started laughing with the police officer. Then she said, 'Where are you all headed, a salad bar?' Dad said he was sorry to be speeding, but his kids were getting ripe and they were starting to draw flies. The officer laughed so hard that she had to take off her dark glasses and wipe tears from her eyes. She finally said, 'Well, get out of here, but go slow! I don't want to find you squashed all over the highway.'"

Chuck had a letter ready for his parents that read, "I know you're real upset right now that I'm going away, but I don't want you to forget this stuff. I don't want you to remember me as being skinny and sick. I want you to think about the good times we had because that's what I remember most."

If you are around people who are concentrating on the negative, encourage them to look for the good. Enjoy today. Feelings of appreciation fill us with happiness and attract positive thinking people into our lives. If only the negative-thinking people of the world could meet a person like Chuck, maybe they would begin to look at the positives in their lives. Maybe they would realize how much they already have—rather than focusing on what didn't go their way. They'd also have more energy, which could help them change things in their lives for the better!

The next time you need to lighten up about a situation, do the following exercise. Get a piece of paper, close your eyes, and draw a picture of your situation with the opposite hand than you would normally write with. Just doing this brings an automatic laugh. Somehow your challenge doesn't look so serious anymore. You've broken a pattern. People begin to overcome their obstacles the moment they start laughing about them. Mark Twain wrote, "Humor is tragedy plus time." The passage of time allows us to look at the situation more objectively. Humor speeds up this process and enables us to move through and beyond our challenges with more ease.

More Ideas to Help You Lighten Up

We've looked at some ideas about how we can all lighten up. Now let's talk about the importance of developing a joyful attitude about life. I ask workshop participants to finish the following statement: "For me to be more humorous, I am waiting for _____." A few samples of their funny lines are:

- ◆ Permission.
- ◆ The coffee to be ready.
- ◆ The barking dog next door to leave town.
- ◆ A better time.
- ◆ My youth to return.
- ◆ A better circle of friends.
- ◆ Spring.
- ◆ You to go first.

If you find you are taking yourself too seriously, here are some things you can do to lighten up:

1. Hang a big picture of your dream vacation, dream house, or dream car on the wall and look at it when you need a mental escape. This also serves as an excellent way to build your dream. It helps you to keep yourself motivated to do whatever it takes to build your profession or business.
2. Take some of the people you lead to a local amusement park to have fun and meet people. Those new acquaintances may later become customers, business associates, and perhaps new friends.

3. Listen to one of your favorite continuing education tapes with a funny story that makes you laugh.

4. Meet some of your employees or business associates at a local zoo. Take photos with the animals! Laugh, build your relationships, and create new ones.

There are also many other attitude adjustment activities that can help you both lighten up and stay motivated as you build your business or career. For example, take some of your staff members or associates to dreambuild—visit some beautiful open houses in the area, drive some exciting cars at a local dealership, or go to a fine restaurant and enjoy a meal. Take some fun photos and laugh a lot. If you aren't yet producing the kind of results you'd like, perhaps in sales, get fired up to make it happen. The dreambuilding may motivate you and your people into making some dreams come true.

This type of relationship-building fun activity could lead to more people getting in the fast lane on the road of success with you. Perhaps they're ready to move on and will start duplicating what you're doing to be successful. And, regardless of what happens afterward, in the process, you'll be adding a new dimension of fun to your life and theirs.

My high school reunion committee had such fun planning a reunion that we decided to get together once a month thereafter. Even though most of us were not close friends in high school, we have a wonderful time together now. We've all made new friends with different and interesting people.

Your friends, family, and business or career associates are likely to sense your excitement of having fun and going *full speed ahead*. Some of them may even want to travel with you on the road of success. Just imagine, you can have an inspiring, life-changing impact on others! And you'll be having more fun on that road as well.

What if you had only two weeks to live! How would you spend your time? Think about the things you love doing. What changes would you make? How can you prioritize your activities to build your business or profession so you can make those changes? Remember, don't postpone joy. Work on adding humor and fun to your life today. Blend fun and pleasure into your business- and career-building activities. Remember to smile today and every day. As someone once said, "Some pursue happiness, others create it." Be one who creates it!

The following article, *If I Had My Life To Live Over—I'd Pick More Daisies*, was originally written by Don Herold. It was then revised by Nadine Stair, reportedly at the age of 85, as below. Much of their advice applies to all of us:

> If I had my life to live over, I'd try to make more mistakes next time. I would relax. I would limber up. I would be sillier than I have been this trip. I know of very few things I would take seriously. I would be crazier. I would take more chances. I would take more trips. I would climb more mountains, swim more rivers, and watch more sunsets. I would have more actual problems and fewer imaginary ones.
>
> You see, I am one of those people who lives sensibly and sanely, hour after hour, day after day. Oh, I have had my moments, and if I had it to do over again, I'd have more of them. In fact I'd have nothing else. Just moments, one after another, instead of living so many years ahead of each day. I have been one of those people who never goes anywhere without a thermometer, a hot water bottle, a gargle, a raincoat, and a parachute.
>
> If I had it to do over again, I would go places and do things and travel lighter than I have. If I had my life to live over, I would walk barefoot earlier in the Spring and stay that way later in the Fall. I would play hooky more. I would ride on more merry-go-rounds. I'd pick more daisies.

I find it intriguing to work with corporations, government agencies, business organizations, and professional associations. I see wonderful programs they create to raise productivity by incorporating fun and humor into their daily activities. They find that people who are having fun in the course of their workday are less likely to be late or absent and are apt to be more productive.

The CEO (Chief Executive Officer) of a huge corporation has a poster on her office door—"Notice! This office requires no physical fitness program. Everyone gets plenty of exercise jumping to conclusions, flying off the handle, running down the boss, tripping people up, dodging responsibility, polishing the apple, and pushing their luck." What a great message to her employees to lighten up. It also points out inappropriate behavior which employees may have believed the CEO didn't notice!

The president of a financial institution notes, "Don't look at me as a boss, but as a friend who is always right." The most down-to-earth, fun-loving people with the best leadership skills get the best results short- and long-term—no question about it. So be a fun-to-be-around person, keep developing your skills and attract others to duplicate what you do. These ideas are keys to staying on the road of success.

The following are some fascinating fun ideas from successful corporations:

♦ Ben and Jerry's Ice Cream Company expects their employees to have a great day—every day. The company encourages their people to have fun on the job. Their attitude is, if it's not fun, why do it? A "joy gang" improves the quality of life for employees and the community. It is a committee which asks what employees need to have to improve the atmosphere at work. In addition, each employee must take three pints of ice cream home daily!

♦ At one of the major airlines in the U.S., flight attendants are recruited for their sense of humor! Sometimes they wear costumes and they even sing their safety regulations. I've seen them in action and they are very funny.

♦ A California dentist took his staff on a field trip to a shopping mall and gave each employee $200. He stipulated that they must buy at least five things, and any money left after the two-hour shopping spree would be returned to him. At the next staff meeting, the employees had a "show and tell" session with their purchases. Imagine the stories and excitement that generated!

♦ Pitney Bowes Corporation, based in Stamford, Connecticut, offers its employees courses in real estate, golf, tailoring, cake decorating, watercolor painting, and photography. What fun!

♦ Bank of America in San Francisco has a "laugh-a-day" challenge for one month. Each employee strives to get their coworkers to laugh each day by sharing cartoons and jokes. The winners of the challenge receive T-shirts and books containing the best jokes and cartoons. Perhaps this helps them gear up to have a great year, full of fun.

◆ The Walt Disney Company opens Disneyland to employees and their families exclusively for one night. Concessions and rides are run by upper management, all dressed in costumes. Besides being a lot of fun, this event allows employees to see the theme park from the customer's perspective.

The list goes on and on. One of my corporate clients covers employees' desks with balloons on their birthdays. A major telephone company in the U.S. uses their own employees in commercials. Management expert and author Tom Peters says, "The number one premise of business is that it need not be boring or dull. It ought to be fun. If it is not fun, you're wasting your life." Many businesses are implementing ingenious ways of helping their people have fun. It's a win-win scenario. The happier the people are at work, the more productive they're likely to be! This same rule applies to entrepreneurs and their business associates as well.

Today, more people are looking for an upbeat environment where they can associate with other positive-thinking people. Often they're tired of the same old routine day in and day out. People who are fired up and having fun are more likely to build a big business or a thriving career. Enthusiasm and fun are contagious.

As Ralph Waldo Emerson once shared, "Nothing great was ever achieved without enthusiasm." And it's likely you want to accomplish great things, or you wouldn't be reading this book. So what better time than *now* to rev up your engine to go *full speed ahead!* Fire yourself up with humor and enthusiasm and share your excitement with others. Help your associates or employees get fired up too! Discover the additional mileage you can get when you add zest and fun to your fine-tuned vehicle.

Talk with a fun-loving role model, perhaps your boss, leader, or whoever you consult with, for their guidance. Ask what you could do to increase your enthusiasm and have more fun with your career or business. These ideas can help you make building your profession or business much more enjoyable. It may be as simple as drawing a smiley face on a 3"×5" index card and taping it to your car dash, as one budding leader did to remind himself to smile!

Actively look for humor in all areas of your life—whether it is on your journey of success in your career or business, or in other aspects of your life. You'll enjoy every day more as you make fun and joy a regular part of your daily experiences. As you move on to create the life you've always wanted, doing more and more of what you love to do, you'll find you will never have to work another day in your life.

Remember the importance of humor. Concentrate on developing your childlike qualities as if you were a kid again. After all, an adult is just a kid in an older body! The idea is to rekindle the child in you. Find delightful, wondrous, and humorous moments whenever you can, in everything you do. You may just need to open your eyes more fully and notice what's happening in your life. Why not record your findings in your day planner or a notebook?

Be kind to yourself—laugh at your shortcomings and mistakes and learn from them. And be sure to take yourself lightly—one of the real keys to creating a happier life. Ask yourself how important the situation you are experiencing today will be in two years. Then resolve it as best you can—and move on.

You don't have to tell a joke to be funny or have fun. For example, next time you go through a highway toll booth, pay for the three cars behind you and drive away, chuckling. Focus on the happy times rather than the sad memories. Associating with positive-thinking people helps tremendously. Ralph Waldo Emerson wrote, "To laugh often and much; to win the respect of intelligent people and the affection of children; to leave the world a better place; to know even one life has breathed easier because you have lived. This is to have succeeded."

Now Implement the *Full Speed Ahead* Action Plan...

Humor is all around us. It waits for us in airports, grocery stores, restaurants, at home, on the job, in our businesses and everywhere else. Go ahead and write down at least one funny incident that you experienced today. It can be a story you heard, something you did (or failed to do), something you saw, something that happened to you, or perhaps a cute cartoon that made you smile.

Start making a habit of keeping track of the humorous times in your life. This will help you focus on the light side, especially during those challenging days we all experience.

Remember that finding humor is a skill. In the beginning it may take you time to notice it. Then, with practice, like anything else, it'll get easier and easier. Once you become good at discovering the humor in your experiences, both you and others will enjoy your great outlook on life!

What five things can you do, starting today, to have more fun in your career or business and in your personal life? Write them down. Make a copy of this list and place it in a prominent location in your home or office. Make sure you do all of the things you have made note of. Be a role model for others to follow and show them how to have fun as they travel on the road of success.

Chapter 5

Communication—It's a Two-Way Street to Build Rapport

"Learn to listen. Opportunity sometimes knocks very softly."
Anonymous

Excellent Communication Is Key to Your Success

People need to communicate—it's a basic human requirement. As infants, from the time we learn to cry, we begin to use our voices as communication tools. As babies we cry because we're hungry or need or want attention. This is communication at its simplest level.

As we grow, communication seems to get more complex and can be confusing, especially if we haven't developed our skills in this area. Yet effective communicators take a tip from infants. They ask for what they want in a direct, clear, and concise way.

Many challenges we experience often result from inadequate, incorrect, or unclear communication. Such difficulties underlie the following list of concerns. Do any of these sound like anything you might say?

- People don't take me seriously.
- People ignore me as if I'm invisible.
- I'm tired of people walking all over me.

♦ I'm too strong and always seem to take over my relationships; I overwhelm other people.
♦ I make all the decisions. I want others to take a stand and decide what to do, for a change.
♦ People misunderstand what I'm trying to say.
♦ I'm afraid of public speaking.
♦ I don't like to meet new people; I'm pretty shy. It's really hard for me when I'm with a lot of people—I feel so uncomfortable.

It's easy to spot patterns here. People, from all walks of life, all over the world, share the desire to communicate so others will listen and understand what they mean. But frequently, clear communication simply doesn't occur. What's the true test? When others act correctly upon what you requested!

Say What You Mean and Mean What You Say

When was the last time a poor communication caused you to lose money, feel embarrassed, or spend extra time getting something done?

The following anecdotes are from the newspaper advertisements and articles. Read them and decide whether the intended message is being heard:

♦ Lost, one small apricot poodle. Neutered. Like one of the family.
♦ Dinner Special—Turkey $2.95; Chicken or Beef $2.25; Children $2.
♦ We don't tear your clothing with machines. We do it carefully by hand.
♦ Wonderful bargains for men with 15 and 17 necks.
♦ German Shepherd, easy to handle, loves to eat anything, especially children.
♦ Persons are prohibited from picking flowers from any but their own graves.
♦ My son is under the doctor's care and should not take physical education today. Please execute him.

These examples show that what we say matters. We need to take great care to say what we mean! Otherwise, we'll spend a lot of time striving to get out of the communication "messes" we've caused!

Conversely, we need to be careful when we accept communication from others. Our office gets at least one call a week from people looking for "speakers" in the classified section of the telephone book, known in the U.S. as the Yellow Pages. They ask, "Do you sell stereo equipment?" They want home or automobile speakers, not a professional speaker. Quite a difference!

The core of communication is *what* you say and *how* others *hear* it. The following are examples of expressions Americans use as jargon:

- ◆ It's as clear as mud. (It's not obvious.)
- ◆ The buck stops here. (It's my responsibility.)
- ◆ Down the drain. (It's wasted.)
- ◆ Ballpark figure. (An estimate.)
- ◆ It won't fly. (It won't work.)
- ◆ It's raining cats and dogs. (A heavy downpour.)
- ◆ Don't make waves. (Don't do anything different.)

Obviously our meaning is not always crystal-clear, judging by the specific words used. Imagine how difficult it must be for people learning English as a second language to understand what we're saying! And to make matters more challenging, most English words have more than one meaning!

The following four skills, to be covered in this chapter, are essential for effective communication:

1. *Active Listening*—Hints to help you better understand what others are saying.
2. *Body Language and Nonverbal Communication*—How others read your mannerisms and actions.
3. *Strategies for Meeting People*—Ideas to help you meet the kinds of people with whom you can create a win-win relationship in your business and personal life.

4. *Presentation Skills*—Learn how to look, sound, and feel confident in front of audiences and in one-on-one situations.

Active Listening

Greek philosopher Epictetus wrote, "Nature gave us one tongue and two ears so we could hear twice as much as we speak." Two statements I hear frequently are, "Listen, opportunity sometimes knocks very softly," and, "If you want me to be a good listener, give me something good to listen to." If all people were excellent communicators, admittedly it would be easier to listen. This points out the need for all of us to communicate as effectively as possible. Then people with poor listening skills will be more likely to hear and understand us!

What don't you like about the way others listen or *don't* listen? Most people dislike it when others talk too much or interrupt when they're speaking. Mark Twain, in his humorous way, once said, "There is nothing so annoying as to have two people go right on talking when you are interrupting!"

Other unskillful behaviors include: avoiding eye contact, never smiling, fidgeting, tapping fingers, picking at nails, finishing sentences for the other person, and arguing. And asking questions about what was just said definitely shows that person was not listening!

As we think about what other people do or don't do that we dislike, we also need to consider our actions that contribute to breakdowns in communication! The root cause of many situations we're faced with is the lack of communication.

I do my best to avoid jumping to conclusions. I've gotten myself into real trouble when I formed an opinion before the other person even finishes communicating his or her message! How about you?

It takes patience to allow the other person to share what's on their mind and heart, especially if it seems to be taking a long time. But it pays off in the long-run. When you truly hear and understand what others are saying, you can avoid obstacles down the road which are caused by initial faulty communication. If exchanges are muddled in the beginning, it takes more time and energy later to straighten it all out!

Here's a letter from a daughter to her parents. I don't know who originally wrote this often-told story that now has a couple of new twists.

Dear Mom and Dad,

I'm sorry for not writing but hope you will understand. First sit down before you read further. I'm doing much better now after recovering from the broken leg I received jumping from the window when my apartment caught fire last month. I can almost walk normally again thanks to the loving care of Tom, the janitor who pulled me from the flames. He more than saved me; he's become my fiancé.

We are planning on getting married in Hawaii and inviting all our friends and family to stay there free for a week with us. You wouldn't mind paying for it all, would you? We haven't set a date yet but will do so shortly. We want to have ten children and live with you, so you can babysit. I knew you would be excited for me, knowing how much you want to be grandparents.

Your loving daughter,
Gail

P.S. There was no fire. My leg is not broken. I'm not getting married, and there is no Tom. However I'm getting an F (failing) in biology class and I wanted you to see that grade in its proper perspective!

I love the following classic story, again with a new twist, which shows the importance of not making assumptions:

An 80-year-old man went to his doctor for a checkup. The doctor told him, "You are in terrific shape. There's nothing wrong with you. Why, you might live forever. By the way, how old was your father when he died?" The patient responded, "Did I say he was dead?" The doctor was astonished. "You mean to tell me you are 80 years old and your father is still alive?" "Not only that," said the patient, "my grandfather is 126 years old and next week he's getting married." "Why on earth does your grandfather want to get married?" asked the doctor.

The patient looked at the doctor and said, "He found a lovely gal, and he wants to start a new family."

Ralph Waldo Emerson wrote, "It's a luxury to be understood." The next time you're actively listening, notice whether you are showing interest in the other person and what they're saying. Are you asking relevant questions that show you're interested? Or are you just waiting for them to pause for a moment, so you can tell *your* story?

I give workshop participants an engaging, yet challenging, exercise. First they separate themselves in pairs. I ask one (the first) partner to talk to the other about a complex situation or disagreement they are experiencing. The person who is listening is instructed not to give advice—only to repeat what the first person is telling them. Most listeners find they need to exert a lot of self-control to just listen and repeat what they hear. Usually the listener wants to jump in and explain how they solved a similar situation. Offering suggestions is appropriate—but only when someone asks for help or is open to your counsel.

Typically, people just want to be heard. They usually know, somewhere deep inside, what they need to do. They may want someone to listen so they can think out loud and reach their own heartfelt conclusions. We need to give them our full attention, so we can correctly hear and understand their message. Then we can ask for clarification, if necessary, when they're finished. Listening is one of the best ways to show you care about other people. It is a key ingredient as you build your career or business and develop bonds with your associates or employees. Listening is loving. So be sure to give your full attention to others, in all areas of your life, to excel in your communications.

Body Language and Nonverbal Communication

Management consultant Peter Drucker wrote, "The most important thing about communication is to hear what *isn't* being said." Baseball legend Yogi Berra said, "You can observe a lot by just watching." The magnitude of these two statements is enormous. In his book *How to Start a Conversation and Make Friends*, Don Gabor shares, "Research has shown that over 70 percent of communication is nonverbal. 'Body Language,' as it is called, often communicates our feelings and attitudes before we speak, and it projects our level of receptivity to others." Nonverbal communication includes what attitudes we are conveying through our gestures, facial expressions, body posture, and tone of voice.

Which has more influence—verbal or nonverbal communication? Many people think communication consists only of words. We need to monitor our nonverbal cues and observe those of others to maximize the effectiveness of our communication. This will help us fix the potholes, replant and freshen up the fallen signs, and avoid unnecessary detours on our road of success.

How's your body language? What do you reveal to others before you even open your mouth? Is it confidence or insecurity, strength or weakness? I realize that, even with the best self-control, the attitude you project may depend on how you're feeling, who you are with, and what you are experiencing that day.

Here's a sentence for you to finish: "When people meet me for the first time they think I am _____." If the answer is shy, and you're really an outgoing, fun-loving person, ask yourself what behavior you could change to more truly reflect your real self. If the answer is aloof, and you are a warm, caring person, look within to find out why people are misreading you.

Ask someone you trust to give you clues to help you be more authentic. Be open-minded and receptive to others in your communications. People are more likely to reach out to those who are flexible and caring, rather than attempt to break down the barriers of those who are rigid and aloof.

Have you ever heard that a person's eyes are the windows to their soul? When you look at a person for just one second you notice him or her as a human being. However, when you look into a person's eyes for three seconds, you notice him or her as an individual. Eye contact helps you to connect emotionally with others. So many people fail in this crucial area—they unthinkingly rush by others in their everyday activities. Always be sure to help others feel that they matter by giving them your full eye contact.

I will always remember a conversation I had with a woman who came up to talk to me at the end of an intense keynote speech. She said, "Joyce, I really loved your words, and I am now aware of roadblocks I have set up in my own life, but you didn't look at me once." Over 1,000 people filled the auditorium and this individual felt neglected. The power of eye contact cannot be overstated.

The tone of your voice also sends a message. People with strong voices get noticed the minute they speak. Those with softer or weaker voices are often ignored. Many people seem to have remote controls in their heads today; if you don't catch their interest early, they just turn you off. We need to capture other people's attention.

Listen to the dynamic leaders in whatever profession or industry you are in. They catch your interest and help you to rise above ordinary thinking. They're fired up and motivating. Their tone of voice reflects passion and conviction. For all of you developing yourself as leaders, you need to be duplicating what those who are successful do. They say what they mean and mean what they say—with dynamic confidence resonating in their voices.

Reflect enthusiasm in your voice. It'll help you attract people with the will to win. This could motivate them to associate with you in your business or career. Some outstanding leaders have had voice lessons to help them sound appealing and credible. Some people use speech coaches to make their voices sound more powerful.

Now take this quiz on verbal and nonverbal communication:

1. Do I realize that just because an idea is clear to me, it doesn't necessarily mean it's clear to someone else?
2. Do I make sure I fully understand what another person has told me before I reply?
3. Am I understanding and respectful of others' feelings, knowing they may feel differently than I do?
4. Am I sensitive to someone else's point of view? Do I make every effort to understand them rather than reacting defensively and being critical?

5. Do I ask questions to clear up any misunderstandings while communicating?
6. Do I understand that once a person feels understood, he or she tends to be less aggressive and defensive?
7. Do I get to know people as individuals? Or, instead, do I tend to prejudge others by their appearance and manner of communicating?

Have you ever given consideration to these questions? (If you said no, you're probably in the majority.) Are you surprised by your answers? Just answering these questions alone, can help many of us achieve a new level of understanding and upgrade our communication skills. Consistently assess your strengths as a communicator, and determine what you need to develop. Become a thoughtful, aware communicator and you'll be in the ranks of the most successful people in the world!

Since your body language and the tone of your voice convey so much about your message, get together with an excellent communicator—perhaps your boss, or whoever is guiding you on your road of success. Ask them what books they could recommend to help you. Such knowledge will help you improve your personal presentation skills and ability to better observe and understand others.

Active listening—and understanding your nonverbal language and that of others—can be the high-octane fuel you need to go *full speed ahead*. Put these skills into practice today! All of us need to monitor and fine-tune our nonverbal language as we meet and communicate with people. The goal is to consistently create win-win scenarios in our business and personal life. We need to be relentless in our pursuit of this goal to create the life we truly want.

Strategies for Meeting People

According to the *American Heritage Dictionary*, a network is defined as, "An extended group of people with similar interests or concerns who interact and remain in informal contact for mutual assistance or support." Networking can range from sharing job leads or prospects, discussing career decisions, referrals for health care, building an organization of independent business owners, and the use of the Internet.

Many people have a fear of networking because they are afraid to talk to new people—they are afraid of being rejected. As rejection expert John Fuhrman says in his book *Reject me—I Love It!*, "Every lasting success involves overcoming rejection. The only reason you may not yet be as successful as you want to be may be because…you haven't been rejected enough!"

To build your career or business, it's essential to develop the skills necessary to meet people and develop relationships. This also applies to your personal life and any professional or entrepreneurial endeavor. You'll always need to meet and deal with people to some degree. Lack of people skills is a common cause for many challenges we face.

You may need to go through a lot of trial and error as you practice meeting people. But it'll be worth it, in the long-run, if you persist and don't give up. We all need to continuously fine-tune our relationship building skills. And, of course, the relationship begins with the first contact you have with someone new.

As children, most of us were taught not to talk to strangers. As we become adults, perhaps go away to college, enter the business community, or attend social functions, we may often find ourselves in a room with people we have never met. There may be cliques. Some may gather in groups and exclude us. Many school-age fears of being excluded may return in adulthood. What do we do?

To make our dreams a reality, we need to overcome and get beyond these fears. We can learn to enjoy meeting people and working with them to create win-win situations. And building a business or profession which requires that we meet a lot of people and build solid, lasting relationships is one of the best ways to do this.

Experts tell us that people are lonely because they build walls around themselves instead of building bridges to each other. When we communicate successfully, we build these bridges. An added ingredient is making connections that enable you to work in association with others, supporting their dreams and helping them reach their goals. This could range from looking for business associates to hiring a new secretary whose dream is to perform administrative work!

A key to picking the ideal candidate is to ask what their dream is. When you find someone who is passionate about what you have to offer—because that's their dream—you've probably found a winner. In the process, you can make your own dreams come alive for yourself and your family. And when you find enough of the dreamers and you help them live their dreams, you'll live yours as well.

Even though the skills required for meeting people are basic, many people are still uncomfortable doing so. Know that you're not alone if you are still tentative about meeting people. Many major leaders in business felt the same way when they began their quest! Some admit that even now, they feel somewhat shy around others. Carry your business cards with you at all times and make sure they contain clear information. You want people to know your name, the name of your business or the name of your employer's business, what you do, and how to contact you.

If you are an entrepreneur and you and your spouse work together in a business, make sure you each have your own business card. (It's more professional and each of you needs your own identity.) Whoever you consult with can answer your questions and make recommendations. Whatever you do, adjust your attitude so you will have fun and a good time. It'll be much easier to meet people that way!

Do you smile easily? If not, you may want to practice doing so. A warm, friendly smile can put others at ease. Here's an idea to consider for those of you who tend to be serious. With a permanent marker, draw a smiley face on four index cards and print "Smile!" under the face. Post these cards in your car, on your bathroom mirror, on your refrigerator, and on your phone at work. It worked for the budding leader I mentioned earlier, and it can help you too.

How's your handshake? Is it limp and unenthusiastic? Or is your grip so powerful that you bruise the other person by cutting off their circulation? For those of you who have very strong hands, you need to be careful not to squeeze other people's hands so hard you hurt them. That would leave a lasting impression alright, but not the appropriate kind. Find a willing participant and practice a firm, comfortable, confident handshake with them. Ask for feedback.

Rehearse a 30-second self-introduction and be ready to use it. If you're going to a builder's show to dreambuild with some of your business associates who aspire to renovate their current home, or build a new one, take this opportunity to meet people. Make a list of questions you want to ask about building or remodeling. This will help you have natural conversations with the vendors and even with the people in the crowd.

As you show an interest in people by asking appropriate questions to learn more about them, you may be sparked to want to continue the relationship. Perhaps they may be good prospects for your business to consider as new associates. Or they might be potential clients or customers who could utilize your products or services. If a potential prospect is in the crowd, you'll want to find out what they do for a living. You can ask if they enjoy their line of work. From their response, you can decide whether to exchange business cards and call them later to talk further. Do not, however, solicit any vendors or patrons on site—this is usually prohibited!

You want to develop strong, healthy, long-lasting relationships in all areas of your life. You'll have lots of chances to practice your listening skills in the process. You want to be clear in your communications and invest in these relationships to create a mutually beneficial liaison. The more you can develop your people skills, the better—for you and everyone else concerned.

Whenever you have an opportunity to meet people to create potential relationships, make sure you mingle with individuals you don't know, instead of always being with people you are familiar with. Practice your leadership skills by being a host, not a guest. You can have this attitude, regardless of whether or not you're the official host. For example, do you know people who are disappointed because they were not introduced to someone they wanted to meet? Don't wait for someone to introduce or greet you. *You* take the initiative. Show a sincere interest in others. As someone once said, "None of the successes of life work unless you do." How true!

Next time you're with people at a gathering, introduce yourself to someone standing all alone. Show an interest in them by asking questions. Then share some things about yourself. But be sure you're focused mainly on them, actively listening to them. You may make a friend for life. You may do business with them at some point. Who knows what could come of it?

People remember those who take an interest in them because most people don't. Many people just talk about themselves rather than focus their attention on others and their needs and wants. Rare is the person who focuses mostly on others in conversation. Recall Emerson's law of compensation, "You must give to receive." Give for the joy of giving and you may be surprised at the bounty of friends you'll make along the way.

Make sure you follow up with people you've met with whom you'd like to do business after the event, session, or meeting is over. Someone has to make the first move. Be that person! Follow the guidelines of the industry you're in as to how to best do that. After gauging your new acquaintance's interest in what you have to offer, it may be appropriate to set a date to get together. Over time you will build relationships with certain people you meet.

There are thousands of success stories of people, who were once strangers, meeting at events and forming long-term mutually beneficial business and personal relationships. This comes from continuously meeting people and following up with them. These ideas could be the missing link for those who have no success in attracting fine, qualified people to associate with. We make our own luck. Use the ideas we discussed to help you prepare for and be successful at meeting such people and creating excellent alliances.

Across the U.S., people ask me for techniques on starting a conversation. It's really quite simple—*just take an interest in other people*. Become other-centered. Smile, say "hi," introduce yourself, and shake hands. If you're a little scared, that's okay— they probably are too, even though they may look confident. Ask open-ended questions that require more than a yes or no answer. This "draws them out" so they can talk while you listen carefully. Here's what an excellent conversationalist does:

♦ Talks on a broad range of subjects and is well informed.

♦ Shows interest in other people personally and in what they do for a living.

♦ Adjusts to the person with whom he or she is talking.

♦ Communicates on *their* level of reception. For example, you wouldn't use industry-specific terminology with someone who isn't in your industry.

♦ Looks straight into the eyes of people they are talking with.

♦ Does not interrupt.

♦ Knows how to pay and accept compliments gracefully.

♦ Helps a shy person feel included in the group.

♦ Is aware when listeners become bored.

♦ Supports people's dreams rather than dampens their enthusiasm with negative comments.

♦ Addresses everyone in the group, i.e., scans the group rather than looking at just one or two people.

♦ Has a great sense of humor and the ability to help people lighten up and have fun. Pokes fun at themselves and situations rather than the people they're talking with.

Here are three examples of how to start a conversation that you can use, or modify as appropriate, if you fear talking with someone you don't know:

1. Make a casual observation, such as, "This is a great turnout. I've never seen so many people attend this event before."
2. Ask a question, like, "Is this your first time here?" or "Are you a member of this organization?"
3. Offer a self-disclosure, like, "I'm really looking forward to hearing today's speakers. I've heard them before and they are dynamic and give valuable information."
4. Give a compliment. Make a sincere positive comment about something, such as the car they drive or their great attitude.

Remember, we need to feel the fear we may have of meeting people and work through it, so we can go *full speed ahead*.

Being visible is another important aspect of meeting people. You could meet your next friend, client, or business associate at a social event, your child's school, a restaurant, in line at the grocery store or bank, or wherever you are during the course of the day. The key is to *always be open to meeting new people and to do it consistently*. You may be pleasantly surprised at what this one commitment to action can do for you on your highway of success!

Did you ever hear the expression, "People don't care how much you know until they know how much you care"? In order to have others find you *interesting*, be *interested* in them. The next time you meet someone, listen while they talk. Let them "clean their slate" and say everything they want to express before you start "writing" on it!

When you take a sincere interest in others, some will tell you their life story! Most people enjoy it when you listen to them. Their favorite topic of conversation is themselves, even if they won't admit it. When they walk away, they'll carry with them the feeling that you're a person they enjoy being around. They'll think you're a great conversationalist, even though *they* did most of the talking!

When they're finished, they'll probably ask about you and your occupation. Just be patient and share sincerely, but don't go overboard. Above all, be more interest*ed* than interest*ing*. Just be yourself, being careful to be genuine. If you try to impress them with your accomplishments, you'll probably turn them off. They may feel "less than" you. Be in the business of building people up—not tearing them down. As British novelist Oscar Wilde once said, "When people are wrapped up in themselves they make a pretty small package." The lesson here is to be wrapped up in others!

Presentation Skills

Fred's face turns red. He is panic-stricken. He is told he must make a speech to his peers. Fred, and many others, experience anxiety when asked to make a toast at a wedding or talk at a child's school function. *One of the greatest keys to success is the ability to make presentations and speak in public.* Here are some simple tips to make these situations easier.

Making a presentation is a learned skill that improves with practice. Some people put their hands in their pockets, to hide their nervousness, when they are called upon to speak in public. A former U.S. President even did that! A very popular U.S. First Lady and United Nations delegate actually fainted at her first speech! But, undaunted, she came back strong.

Presenters admit to a wide range of mistakes. Inappropriate teasing is one—such as the speaker who told lawyer-bashing jokes without realizing the CEO and the president of the company were both attorneys! It's a safer bet to tell appropriate jokes that don't discriminate against anyone. Poke fun at yourself, not others.

Talking too quickly or too slowly also alienates audiences. You could put people to sleep if you talk too slowly. A lack of enthusiasm and a monotone voice bore people. Be excited about what you have to share. Not having enough knowledge about your topic is usually very apparent. So do your homework ahead of time!

You can avoid these dilemmas and make presentations, big or small, successfully. Here are my favorite strategies for preparing and making powerful and successful presentations:

- ♦ **Know and care about your audience.** Place the spotlight on the source of what is probably your biggest anxiety— your audience. Ask some of them, perhaps beforehand, their reason for being there. Understand their needs, their challenges, and their dreams and goals. Be confident you have something of great value to share.

- ♦ **Build rapport.** How are you and your audience alike? Have you all just driven there in a snowstorm? Were you, yourself, in the audience just a short time ago? If so, share it. When people have things in common with you they tend to feel more comfortable because they can relate to you better. So be genuine and share sincerely.

♦ **Have fun.** Put some clean, non-ethnic, non-political and non-sexist jokes on some index cards and share them with the audience. This will help relax both you and your audience. So what if you're not an expert at telling jokes? It's a good time to practice. Poke fun at yourself and something you did that relates to your audience's circumstances.

♦ **Understand your fear.** Being nervous is normal. Others are nervous too, but some hide it better than others. Focus on the audience and watch your fear go away. The fear generally comes from focusing on our anxieties. Once you focus on your audience and on how you can help them, your fears will melt away. Ask for help on this if you need it.

♦ **Relax before, during, and after the presentation.** Take a deep breath and look at the people in your audience before you say your first word. This relaxes you and shows you have control, even though the "butterflies" may be fluttering in your stomach. No one can see what's going on inside you.

♦ **Organize your talk.** Your audience will appreciate an orderly presentation. Use note cards if you need to. Be sure to number them to keep them in order, just in case you drop them on the floor by mistake!

♦ **Know your purpose.** Are you going to inform, inspire, or persuade? It might be all three. You want the audience to be happy they came to hear you. Take the opportunity to meet them afterward. Imagine that on their forehead are the initials "MMFI"—Make Me Feel Important. Your job is to do that by sharing your ideas, your opportunity, or your products and services.

The opening of your presentation could comprise approximately 15 percent of your time, the body 75 percent, and the closing remarks about 10 percent. Use your opening remarks to grab their attention and build trust and credibility. Add interesting elements to "hook" the audience. Create a need in their mind for the information you'll be presenting. For example, if you're sharing a business concept, talk about the aspirations and challenges the audience might have that this new idea may help them reach or resolve. An industry expert or your mentor can be a valuable resource in preparing your presentation.

If you're part of a team, attend other people's presentations, take notes, and ask permission to tape record the talk. Be a student of what you're doing. Be teachable, no matter what your level of success, even though you may feel you have reached the peak level of expertise. Remember what it took to get to that point? You may be in a new situation now. Be patient with yourself as you stretch in a new direction—perhaps to take more of a leadership role in your job or business.

In the body of your speech use facts, quotes, challenging questions, and personal stories to make your points. Give facts that show you know more than your audience. However, if someone asks a question you can't answer, honestly admit it and tell your audience you will seek the answer. In your closing remarks, summarize, tie back into the opening, and suggest that your listeners take action.

The most significant aspects of making a presentation are: Be yourself, focus on the people you're sharing with, and talk to them like they're your friends. Be other-centered and reach out to them, and your fear of speaking will disappear. Ask your boss or other expert to recommend books and tapes on this most important skill.

Being able to make effective presentations can enhance your personal life too. There will be toasts to make at weddings, fun presentations to make at get-togethers, honoring people at landmark birthdays, anniversaries, and the like. Your friends and relatives will be there, rooting for you. You are a unique person with a special message to give others. Show that you care about the honoree, and perhaps recall a funny story of being together. Be prepared. You have more to give than you may realize.

Clear communication is essential to excel in all areas of life. And active listening alone will upgrade your relationships with others. People love to be heard.

What else is more important than our relationships and how we choose to contribute to the world through them? One of life's biggest challenges is how to best share our love for people. This can only be done by being yourself and working with and through others. Learning how to clearly communicate is most certainly a key element.

Be interested in others, and they'll find you more interesting! Notice your body language. Is it open and relaxed? Meeting and building relationships with others provides great opportunities to develop your communication skills. You'll learn as you go along. Feel the fear and work through any anxiety the next time you make a presentation, meet people at an event, or as a part of your everyday activities. You can do it!

Be assured that many industry leaders, as comfortable and proficient at speaking as they are now, didn't start out that way. Some of them found that overcoming their fear of speaking to a group (or even one-on-one) was one of the biggest hurdles they had to overcome to be successful. They made a conscious decision to get out of their comfort zone and do it. Their success depended upon it, and most likely, so does yours.

In order to achieve your personal best and make your dreams a reality, you need to get up just one more time than you fall. Look for and take opportunities to meet new people. Take your staff or business associates out to meet people. Make it a fun experience by dreambuilding at the same time. Show others how interested you are in them. Be brave and make new presentations. Don't wait for your ship to come in. Swim out to it—the water's fine! Go *full speed ahead!*

Now Implement the *Full Speed Ahead* Action Plan...

This section will help you think about how you communicate with others face-to-face. Read the entire list, then circle or highlight the skills you would like to improve on. Tackle them one at a time, and encourage others to do the same.

- ◆ Be brief, concise, and get to the point.
- ◆ Be assertive and definite—rather than hesitant and apologetic.
- ◆ Talk in specifics—give examples and details.
- ◆ Tell compelling personal stories—give people hope and understanding. Encourage others to do the same.

♦ Let others know when you don't understand something they've said. Don't pretend you get their point and gloss over it. Admit it if you weren't listening and became distracted.

♦ Let others know when you like something they have said or done—compliment them.

♦ Don't argue with others. You may win the battle but you'll lose the war. Be open-minded. Listen to their point of view—you may learn something.

♦ Accept people unconditionally. Look at what they can be. And do the same for yourself.

♦ Listen to understand, rather than thinking about your next remark. Be totally focused on others and their message.

♦ Ask others what they are thinking and feeling, rather than assuming you know.

♦ Stay with others emotionally—supporting them and allowing them to feel your caring empathy.

♦ Talk in group discussions—participate rather than being passive.

♦ Be able to tolerate silence with others. Know that silence is golden and that you don't need to be talking in order to be comfortable.

♦ Accept help from others with gratitude.

♦ Stand up for yourself while maintaining self-control.

What ideas will you use from this chapter? Write them down. Make a copy of this plan and place it in a prominent location where you'll see it every day—on your refrigerator, for example.

Top performers are people who realize they need to express their feelings. They confront ambiguity by asking questions for clarification. They take responsibility for their relationships by communicating in a direct and open style. What are your strengths when communicating with others? Go ahead and list them.

Chapter 6

Diversity—Even Cadillacs, Hondas, Mercedes, and Chevys Can All Get Along

*"Variety is an essential ingredient in life; everyone's different.
Accept people as they are, don't find fault. Different equals different.
Different does not equal wrong."*
Joyce Weiss

Appreciate the Differences in Others

Picture a world filled with people just like you. They look identical to you, have the same skin tone, hair color, and eyes. They're the same height, the same sex, age, and share the same talents, skills, interest, and hobbies. What kind of world would this be? Boring! Living in a homogeneous world wouldn't work—there would be no balance or variety. Yet some people seem to want just that—everyone to be just like them!

To achieve the success we are capable of, personally and professionally, we need to appreciate the differences in each other. That statement sounds simplistic. And it is simple. But simple doesn't necessarily mean it's always easy.

Appreciating diversity is recognizing, valuing, and using the unique talents and contributions of all individuals, regardless of their differences. These could include—race, gender, age, language, height, weight, physical and mental abilities/challenges, religion, technical/nontechnical skills, income level, marital status, education, geographical background, residential location, birth order, values, work longevity, or even eating habits. Can you add to this list?

We are often different, even when we look the same, by virtue of our various value systems. Do your best to understand others who are different from you. At times, people put on blinders and don't face the realities of their prejudice. This chapter is a mini-version of my diversity workshop which I've presented around the U.S.

The population is changing and these changes will have a significant impact on everyone. For example, during the 1970s, in the U.S., the average worker was 29 years old, male, white, local, and married with children.

Women of that time generally worked in the home or part-time elsewhere. Those women who worked outside the home were usually teachers, nurses, or secretaries. Older workers were considered smarter, and people with physical or mental challenges were not routinely found in the workplace.

Today, only 7 to 10 percent of the families in the U.S. fit the traditional American model of a father who works, a mother who stays at home, and 2.4 children. As we began the new millennium, white males were predicted to comprise only 15 percent of incoming employees. And about 60-65 percent of females over the age of 16 worked outside the home.

Today women make up nearly 50 percent of the workforce, contrasted with 30 percent in 1950. These women are likely to place their children in day-care centers. Employers who want to remain competitive during the 21st century will need to understand the unique needs of their ever-changing workforce. By understanding and appreciating diversity, and including everyone, companies will increase their bottom line (profits).

Once the U.S. was known as the melting pot of the world. This view has proved to be inaccurate. Not only is it impossible to melt or fuse together the many diverse groups that make up the U.S. population, many individuals are not willing to blend.

For example, there are groups of people sprinkled throughout the U.S. who share the same heritage—and prefer to live and associate with each other. They may or may not speak English and they often carry on the cultural rituals of their home country in food preparation, clothing, and such. These individuals represent a minority of people, yet, nonetheless, it proves that a melting pot is truly the wrong metaphor!

Everybody's Different

Instead of a melting pot, picture the U.S. as a healthy tossed salad—a fresh, wonderful collection of colors, textures, and flavors. When everything is blended together, the ingredients are still distinctive.

No matter what country you live in, it's probably comprised of different minorities retaining their own identities. Therefore, we need to be sensitive to each other's needs. We need to treat *all* people with respect and dignity as individuals.

Many challenges are generated in today's business world because some people are still playing the old "we versus they" game. The more we are able to regard others as valuable human beings— different in some ways, yet still an important part of the whole— the better off we'll be. If we consider certain people less than or better than we are, unnecessary conflict between people is created. These old attitudes detract from successful team building ideals.

People differ in numerous ways. As individuals we were formed by a complex blend of variables—our ancestors' value systems, personalities, energy levels, and much more. Even siblings who grew up in the same house can be quite different. Each person has their own distinct personal history and can contribute to the good of the world in their own special way.

Different Equals Different

Different equals different. Different does not equal wrong. Workshop participants share with me how this statement helps them cope in this changing world.

Businesspeople who hope to thrive in this 21st century need to think about the importance of diversity. Forward-looking businesspeople know that a good mix of employees and business associates can increase their bottom line.

The customer base is also changing. Businesspeople need to be aware of and provide for the diverse needs of not only their employees but their customers as well.

Cutting edge companies lead the way in diversity. They know that one key to their success is a good combination of satisfied people, whether they're staff, associates, customers, or clients. They put people first. It may require more effort but pays off in the long-run.

New studies compare companies comprised of a diverse workforce with those that aren't. The results aren't surprising. A diverse workforce increases sales, growth, and performance.

Companies with a vision are teaching their people that differences can provide valuable resources. Just think how many family relationships would improve if a greater number of relatives would be more accepting of each other, instead of making rash judgments and wounding the self-esteem of other family members.

Diversity Ground Rules

Consider these ground rules on diversity for use at home, in your community, and in your business or profession:

- ◆ There are few totally right or totally wrong answers.
- ◆ Listen to each other.
- ◆ Respect the differences in others.
- ◆ Agree that it is okay to disagree.
- ◆ Speak for yourself.
- ◆ Contribute honestly and positively.
- ◆ Have fun.
- ◆ Different equals different. Different does not equal wrong.

I once had the pleasure of sharing the speaking platform with Olympic gold medal gymnast Mary Lou Retton. Her coach, Bela Karolyi, also coached Romanian gymnast Nadia Comaneci. Mary Lou explained how the coach had to learn to treat her and Nadia differently because they were two distinct people. Mary Lou drew energy from the spotlight and the applause. She was fired up by competing with others in the Karolyi gym, whereas Nadia was motivated by her passion for excellence rather than the encouragement from the crowd. These two different women each needed a unique approach from their coach so he could bring out their best.

Learning the Needs of Others

We need to treat others the way they want to be treated, not how we think they "should be" treated based on our own preferences. We also need to express our individual needs before we can expect to have them met. To assume people know what we want can lead to a lot of disappointments—as you may have already discovered.

We benefit by learning the needs of the people we live with, associate with in the community, and build our business or career with. Although challenging to accomplish, it is definitely worth doing. Many things, that were formerly unclear to us, can reveal themselves when we understand and appreciate others' differences.

Let's concentrate on some challenges we face when we are with people different from ourselves. Without thinking about it, we may often judge, show prejudice, and stereotype other people—all of which slows our personal and professional growth, and negatively impacts others.

Judging Others

We may make rash judgments about people and situations before we have enough information. We may "fill in the blanks" haphazardly, because we're in a hurry and don't want to invest the time needed to learn more.

My husband, Jerry, once told me a story about a man who was stranded in the desert and desperately looking for water. He came upon a salesman yelling, "Ties for sale, ties for sale." The thirsty man thought the tie salesman was peculiar but, nonetheless, he continued on his way searching for water. The next day, the thirsty man, crawling on hands and knees, weak and unable to walk, encountered the salesman again, shouting, "Ties for sale, ties for sale." By now the man was so weak he totally ignored the salesman. Suddenly he saw a restaurant on the horizon. The man crawled inside and was greeted by the host who announced, "You will need a tie, sir, before we can serve you." How often do we make judgments before we know all the facts? Enjoy the following essay, author unknown, titled, "First Thoughts":

"You and I, we meet as strangers, each carrying a mystery within us. I cannot say who you are. I may never know you completely, but I trust that you are a person in your own right, possessed of a beauty and value that are the Earth's richest treasures. So I make this promise to you; I will impose no identities upon you, but will invite you to become yourself without shame or fear. I will hold open a space for you in the world and allow your right to fill it with an authentic vocation and purpose. For as long as your search takes, you have my loyalty."

I usually read this essay at the beginning of a training session, which prompts an interesting discussion. One man explained how his company judged him negatively because he doesn't play golf. He invests his evening hours building his home-based business, so he can afford to have his wife stay at home to take care of their disabled child. Yet he knows that some of his peers joke about him. They don't relate to someone who chooses not to play golf. They don't ask questions to understand why, either. Instead, they choose to poke fun at the man.

Another person said she is a vegetarian and brings tofu to work. She is ridiculed as a health nut. Her coworkers are not aware of the fact that she has cancer and is experimenting with a new diet.

Betty used to be very critical of others. She couldn't sleep well, had stomachaches, and was angry most of the time. She sought a counselor for help. Her first and most challenging task was to stop judging others. When she ceased criticizing others, her stomachaches and sleeping problems subsided. Her circle of friends is beginning to grow because she now accepts differences and, most importantly, she accepts herself. What an important lesson she learned—we didn't all come over on the same ship, but in many ways, we are all in the same boat—humankind.

Do you ever feel badly for being different or unique? Recently I was challenged by a moment of doubt about my own uniqueness. I was being myself and having a great time at a dinner party. I was energetic, acting a little "off the wall," and a bit zany. Unexpectedly, one of the guests said, "Joyce, chill!" My interpretation of what that person said was, "Joyce, you're too much, too strong, too passionate, too intense!" I internalized this, starting to doubt myself.

Several days later my daughter was thanking me for the "gifts" I have passed onto her—her raspy voice, her Mr. Magoo (poor) vision, her bow legs, and her addiction to chocolate. I said, "Wendy, tell me something good that I have given you." She whispered in my ear, "Your intensity, Mom." I said, "Seriously, Wendy, tell me one good thing." She replied, "Mom, my intensity made me valedictorian of my high school class, earned me several promotions at work, and gives me the passion, commitment, and perseverance to go after my dreams."

Suddenly my self-doubts began to vanish. I realized my uniqueness is the greatest gift I have. Know what your uniqueness is. Trust that it is your strength and make it an ever-present, vital part of your life. Different equals different. Different does not equal wrong.

To raise your level of compassion...
- Set aside snap judgments.
- Understand and remind yourself of your positive qualities and why others may appreciate them.
- Give yourself permission not to agree with or approve of everything you see. Yet do your best to suspend judgment until you learn more.
- Be open-minded, expand your view, and gain insight.

Prejudice

I ask workshop participants if they have experienced any kind of prejudice. Almost everyone raises their hand. After we establish trust among the group, the discussion usually becomes very intense. People learn they may look and sound different, but they share common experiences.

The following attitudes can signal prejudice you may be experiencing in your personal and business life:

♦ The world consists of us and them.

♦ We are right; they are wrong.

♦ We are good; they are bad.

♦ We are beautiful; they are ugly.

Prejudice thrives on hatred, fear, and ignorance—while pretending innocence. In contrast to the amazing technological advances of the past hundred years, the levels of understanding and compassion for others with differences has not kept pace. Discrimination and oppression are still present throughout the world. Have you ever noticed those symptoms of prejudice in yourself? In your friends? It takes courage to admit it. But that's the first step to overcoming prejudice. If you said yes, then maybe it's time for a tune-up. Prejudicial attitudes and behaviors will not serve us now or in the future.

People are becoming more aware; the world is changing. Let's all be a part of the positive change, as role models of compassion and understanding. You may be thinking, "What I do isn't important; I'm just one person." Not true! You play a bigger role than you may think. What your attitudes are, and what you say and do, affects others around you. So let's all make our impact a positive one!

Here's a simple, yet effective, approach to help you deal with a friend or business acquaintance who uses inappropriate language that reflects an attitude of discrimination: "I really care about you as a friend. I would appreciate it if you would not use those words when I am with you." Help make the other person aware that such prejudicial expressions or words are not acceptable in today's diverse world. As Will Rogers wrote, "We will never have true civilization until we have learned to recognize the rights of others."

Stereotypes

Stereotypes don't appear out of nowhere. Many times they come from our upbringing and old family habits of thinking and behavior. They are based on beliefs that certain people who are different than we are will automatically have certain characteristics and behaviors. Stereotypes induce negative feelings, block out information, and cloud judgment. We may cling to them for convenience—avoiding the effort it takes to learn about someone we don't understand.

We can overcome stereotyping by being nonjudgmental, and more accepting. Instead of typecasting, make opportunities to listen and pay attention to people as individuals, rather than labeling them according to preconceived notions.

Stereotypes get in the way of diversity in organizations and every other arena. Some people don't want to change and don't understand why it is necessary to get along better with others. Some people will not change until they are forced to do so. They may like the status quo. Why rock the boat when they believe their way has always worked in the past?

One book or one workshop will not erase stereotypes, judgment, and prejudice. Time and effort are required to change attitudes that have often been with us since childhood. Realizing that "my" way may not be the only way is a monumental task for some, especially those not schooled in personal development. Fortunately, though, we *can* change our thinking and behavior.

Adult attitudes often promote stereotypes—especially among young people. We influence future generations, whether we realize it or not. If we criticize our children, they learn to condemn. If they live with hostility, they learn to fight. Yet, when we teach our children tolerance, they are more likely to be patient. When we teach them security, they learn to have faith in themselves and others. When we teach them friendliness, our children learn that the world has many people who will respond in kind to their friendliness—even those who are considered difficult people.

Some of us grew up with parents who encouraged us to expand our friendships beyond our small circle of friends and to learn from the great variety we encounter. Others instilled fear by limiting their children's associations to their homogeneous group.

Attitudes take time to change—depending on the motivation level of the person. Some people absolutely refuse change. The newspapers report about radical groups, like terrorists and clans that still exist today, while displaying blatant prejudice. Visualize a bright future for our changing world. What can we do, as individuals and groups, to insure peace and harmony? First, we can monitor our own attitudes and behavior to eliminate any prejudicial tendencies. Then we can encourage others to do the same.

We have looked at existing challenges and some of the options we have to make a positive difference. Now we need more specific strategies to effect necessary change. These tips will help you deal with an inappropriate joke or being in the minority group at a social or business function.

Sometimes you will be in the dominant culture or group. Will you consistently be open-minded, realizing and appreciating that others have fresh ideas and different perspectives to bring to your life or organization? Will you open your eyes and heart to embrace the gifts they bring? Will you coach others, of all backgrounds and differences, on how to succeed? Will you apologize if you have offended someone from a different background or with some other difference?

It's likely there will be other times when you will not belong to the dominant group. If you are rejected, will you understand that this just means you need to go in another direction? Will you still maintain your self-esteem? Will you be alert and open to learning new information and skills to succeed with a broad spectrum of people? As you learn about people who are different than you, will you share that knowledge with those who are more like you? Will you resist blaming any particular group, dominant or otherwise, for everything that goes wrong? Will you be the first to offer your hand and your smile and ask, "What can I do to make things better? How can I make a difference?"

Care About People Who Are Different from You

Some people consider themselves change agents. They challenge others who tell jokes at the expense of another group of people. They refrain from repeating rumors that reinforce prejudice. They avoid generalizations like "all blacks/whites are...," "all disabled are...," or "all men/women are...."

Change agents care about people different from themselves. They understand people need to be encouraged rather than put down. They risk acceptance to say and do what they feel is right, regardless of whether others agree or not. They are true to themselves and their own values. Are you a change agent? If not, will you stand up and become one?

Champions for change ask for an explanation of racist or other inappropriate jokes—they encourage people to think about what they're doing when they tear others down. They push for the explanation until people are uncomfortable. Usually the person telling the offensive joke will avoid doing so in the future, if just to avoid another confrontation. Others discuss it privately with the other person when they feel a joke or comment was improper and hurtful.

No matter how you handle the situation, the most important thing is to not let inappropriate behavior continue; *do something.* Do it firmly and kindly, just as you would want to be dealt with. This may require some practice.

If you leave the room in the middle of an inappropriate story or joke, the person telling the joke will usually get the hint. You could hint by saying "ouch" when a person says something distasteful. People need to know when they are being offensive— some may not even realize it, they've been doing it for so long. Will Rogers said, "I don't think I ever hurt any man's feelings by my little gags. I know I never willfully did it. When I have to do it to make a living, I will quit."

On the Light Side—Political Correctness

Some people are fed up with politically correct language. At times people can go too far trying to make every expression acceptable to everyone. The following examples are taken from comments I have heard that were intended to make sure we are politically correct. These may seem humorous to you. Sometimes the realities of life are much funnier than any material humorists can come up with!

Real estate is an industry that requires great sensitivity in how their advertising is done to avoid discrimination. They must comply with the *Fair Housing Manual.* These are not jokes. They are actual situations I have heard realtors share in my workshops. There's a hefty price to pay for non-compliance. Breaking the law can cost the realtor $50,000!

They can't advertise that a house is "near a church" because someone reading the ad might think only churchgoers are acceptable buyers. They're prohibited from saying, "Large yard—perfect for children." People who don't have children may feel it's discrimination. The term "walk-in closet" can no longer be used because people who are unable to walk may perceive that they can't use it.

It seems that virtually everyone who advertises anything needs to be on the alert for avoiding discriminatory language. For example, if a female student looking for a female roommate writes "no drug addicts," she risks a fine. Drug addiction is considered a disability under both federal and state law. And the list goes on....

Driving Toward Acceptance and Appreciation

Person by person, group by group, the world is changing and organizations that train their people on sensitivity and diversity will gain global appeal. Celebrate events that honor diversity. At the day's end, reflect on the diverse events and people in your life. Learn to appreciate these differences and the excitement and variety they contribute to your life. Use change and diversity as a wonderful opportunity to learn and grow.

No one's attitudes and behavior are perfect, and old biases may slip out of our mouths occasionally. If so, we need to apologize and set a positive example for those around us. Be aware of your own prejudices and understand their origins. Challenge yourself to examine your negative assumptions and beliefs about people who are different than you—then make the necessary changes. You'll be opening up a whole new exciting world for yourself by broadening your perspective—consider it a great adventure!

Nature's beauty comes in all colors. And, similarly, the strengths of humankind take many forms. Every human being is wonderfully unique. All of us contribute in different ways. When we learn to honor the differences, and appreciate the mix, we'll find harmony, greater success, and peace of mind.

Now Implement the *Full Speed Ahead* Action Plan...

Determine your attitude toward diversity and change by taking a few moments to respond to these questions, checking either yes or no.

	Yes	No
1. Do you challenge others privately when they make racially, ethnically, or otherwise offensive comments?	____	____
2. Do you challenge people publicly when they make fun of others because of their race, gender, ethnic background, religion, appearance, disability, or other differences?	____	____
3. Do you think about the impact of your comments and actions before you speak or act?	____	____
4. Do you avoid language that reinforces stereotypes, such as "You're acting like wild Indians!" "Jew them down," "White of you," and "I'll get my girl to do it"?	____	____
5. Do you learn about people different from yourself, by reading, attending seminars, and watching educational TV specials?	____	____
6. Do you value people who are different from you as a resource because of their unique skills, abilities, perspectives, and approaches?	____	____
7. Do you look beyond physical characteristics, disabilities, attractiveness, height, weight, and dress, when interacting with others and making decisions about their ability?	____	____

Write down a plan for how you will use the new ideas you learned from this chapter. Make a copy of your plan and place it in a prominent location in your home or office. Do all of the things you have made note of within 24 hours, if possible.

Top performers are people who realize the value of team building. They understand and appreciate the benefits of being with people who are different from themselves. What groups do you belong to where team members are different from you? How have these differences been beneficial to you?

Chapter 7

Creativity—Discover the Back Roads to Develop Your Creative Genius

"Creativity is not the exclusive property of geniuses, but a set of skills and habits anyone can develop. It's not about where one works; it's about giving oneself permission to be creative."
Joyce Weiss

The Best Can Only Get Better

Creativity is the ability to look at the same things everyone else does, but to see them in another way—to find the hidden connections between the facts and create something different or completely new. It could be as easy as changing the lens or focus on your camera. It could also be something as grand as a classical symphony, or as simple as a new way to arrange your desk to be more productive.

In order to succeed in today's competitive and fast-paced society, we need to see and do things differently than we have ever done before. You may be thinking everything seems just fine at home or with your business or profession. I challenge you to find the things in your life that, with some creativity, might be improved, and to take action to make it happen!

A corporation president once said, "It's a marathon race. Some people will sail across the finish line. Others will fall by the side of the road." I remember an interview I heard from the Summer Olympics in Barcelona, Spain. A commentator asked an athlete why she had changed her strategy in the middle of the event. The commentator was surprised because the athlete always ran her race the same way; her method was tried and tested. She replied, "I got here, looked at my competition, and knew if I did my best I wouldn't be among the winners."

Adopt the philosophy that the best can only get better. As a wise person once said, "It's what you learn after you know it all that counts!" Give your all to everything you do today, then someday you'll be able to do anything you want.

This chapter will help you find and use your creativity to enrich the lives of others which, in turn, will benefit your life. These ideas can be used in both your personal and professional life. Creativity will spice up your existence and can help to improve the morale of those you associate with, in all areas of your life.

During my workshops, only a few people usually raise their hands when I ask the question, "How many of you are creative?" Some people assume they have to be artistic and draw, paint, sculpt, sew, or write poetry to be creative. But we are all born with creativity. *The magic inside you is no hocus pocus. Set your goals and you create the focus.* Does this statement look familiar by now?

Creativity is not the exclusive property of geniuses, but an outlook, a set of skills and habits anyone can develop. The people willing to question ineffective rules, and then look for other more workable options, are more likely to succeed. They are the innovators—those on the cutting edge of positive change. They're the ones who escape the rut of boredom and mediocrity.

Here's another example of creativity: A plain iron bar is worth $5. If you forge horseshoes from that iron bar, the value increases to $10.50. If it is made into needles, the price rises to $3,285. And, if you make watch springs from it, its worth increases to a whopping $250,000! The difference between $5 and $250,000 is creativity!

What stops some of us from pursuing creativity? You've probably heard some of these excuses from negative-thinking people:

- It won't work.
- A leopard can't change its spots.
- Who do you think *you* are?
- If it were possible, someone else would have done it.
- You can't teach an old dog new tricks.
- If it's so good, how come everybody isn't doing it?
- What will happen if the project fails?
- Just let it be—don't rock the boat.
- Yes, but...
- We tried that before.
- We've always done it that way.
- I don't have the time.
- Don't waste time thinking.
- That's really a stupid idea.
- Don't be ridiculous.
- I don't get paid to think.
- That's not in my job description.
- Your idea is too far ahead of the times.

In most cases, these are creativity-stopping, dreamstealing phrases. Upon hearing them, people use them as excuses to put a halt to their creative thinking and dreaming. They allow negative thinking, non-creative people to shut them down. Even if someone says "I tried that once before and it didn't work," it doesn't matter. They're not you and probably don't have the dream you do. You need to be open-minded and do whatever it takes to follow your dream—no matter what anybody else may think, say, or do.

The following is a real-life story that shows the importance of pursuing your creative ideas. A bright young man once wrote about a potential venture he created as an assignment for a college business course. The professor wrote on the paper, "Your ideas are too unrealistic; please stick to your guidelines for the project." Fred Smith, the creator and founder of Federal Express, was the student. His idea was to deliver mail within 24 hours. Today, his service provides an important asset to businesses throughout the world. He didn't let this professor destroy his idea. He took responsibility and ran with it.

In 1905 Ernest Hamwi sold waffles at the World's Fair. When he noticed people were getting bored and wanted something new, he folded his waffles and put ice cream inside. The rest is history.

There are thousands of stories like these. One could be yours. Remember to keep the creative juices flowing—especially when someone tries to sabotage your idea. Naysayers have tried to squash many a newborn idea. It has happened repeatedly in my life, and perhaps in yours, too.

Years ago, people chided me and said I would never be successful as a professional speaker because I was a woman and the profession was, in their opinion, too new. People said speaking was not a "real" job and I would be wasting my time and energy. Today more than 4,000 professional speakers in the U.S., both male and female, belong to the National Speakers Association.

A speaking career is one of the many ways to contribute to society; we help people achieve their goals and succeed in life. I'm glad I followed my dreams, regardless of what the critics said! As American writer David Thoreau wrote, "If you have built castles in the air, that is where they should be; now put foundations under them." Prove the critics wrong and follow your dreams too. As someone once said, "There are no statues erected to critics."

People often place mental blocks in their way that inhibit their creativity. Let's look at some examples:

Mental Block 1—*Follow the Rules*

Sometimes we become more creative by questioning the rules if they don't make sense to us. (In some cases, we may need an explanation because we don't understand the reasoning behind the rule.) Polish astronomer Copernicus questioned and disproved the theory that the earth was the center of the universe. Napoleon found another way to fight a successful military campaign. Twentieth century Spanish artist Pablo Picasso conceived another use for the bicycle; he removed the seat and handle bars and welded them together to create his famous bull sculpture.

Many people, as children, were taught not to color outside the lines. As adults, they translated that to mean not to venture outside of what's commonly done and to follow the crowd. The challenge here is that, to be successful, we need to think "outside the box" and go in the direction that's truly best for us. What's right for us isn't necessarily what most people are thinking and doing. In many cases, there's more than one right answer. Time is moving on and so are we—with creativity.

Most people feel more comfortable following the rules than challenging them. They often fear rejection or disapproval of some kind.

Some professionals in today's unemployment lines still firmly believe that keeping a low profile and not making waves are the best ways to keep your job. But times have changed. Businesses depend on innovation. To succeed they need to look at new ways of doing things.

For example, the distribution of products and services has expanded to global proportions via the Internet. People who are tied into such distribution capacity can maximize their productivity through technology. Some direct sales organizations are taking giant steps in this direction, as well as countless other companies on the cutting edge of cyberspace creativity. Such innovation not only improves distribution, but gives the average person a chance to really excel in life.

I know a very talented woman who was asked to leave her company. Management told her she had all "the right stuff" to make it there, but she didn't venture beyond the rules to offer any creative alternatives. They wanted employees with the courage to think independently. They gave her job leads and an outstanding reference. They knew that in order for their company to survive and thrive, they needed creative employees.

Keep asking yourself how you can develop your skills and talents better. You may be at the top of your success ladder, and I send my congratulations.

However, realize that to keep your edge—to stay fresh and forward thinking—you need to be constantly growing and fine-tuning yourself. You need to be on a continuing education program of books, tapes, and seminars to stay motivated and upgrade your knowledge.

There really isn't any such thing as status quo. You're either moving ahead or falling behind. Time's moving on, so if you're not growing yourself, you're going backward!

Dare to be creative, and as you do, remember the following words. They were written years ago by an insightful person who knew the inherent risks of living a full, creative life:

> "To laugh is to risk appearing a fool. To weep is to risk appearing sentimental. To reach out for another is to risk exposing your true self. To place your ideas, your dreams before the crowd is to risk their loss. To love is to risk not being loved in return. To live is to risk dying. To hope is to risk despair. To try is to risk failure.
>
> But risks need to be taken because the greatest hazard in life is to risk nothing. The person who risks nothing does nothing, has nothing, is nothing. He may avoid suffering and sorrow, but he simply cannot learn, feel, change, grow, love...live. Chained by his beliefs, he is a slave; he has forfeited freedom. Only a person who risks is free."

Mental Block 2—*Be Realistic*

Being realistic can sometimes have its place. Some people use it as an excuse to stay stuck.

Think about the following questions and have fun discussing them in group situations: What if people were born old and grew young? What if electromagnetic disturbances made all radio and television reception impossible? What if dogs or cats were more intelligent and kept people as pets?

These "what if" questions are unrealistic, yet they start people thinking differently—beyond their normal patterns. They can spark new creativity and insight. They shake any mental cobwebs we may have from thinking "inside the box"!

In the 1800s flight was considered unrealistic, and then the Wright Brothers started believing. Even though most of the world still thought it was unrealistic, Wilbur and Orville believed in it so much that they invented the airplane.

Always remember that "realistic" is whatever you can think of and believe—and whatever you believe, you can accomplish!

Mental Block 3—*To Err Is Wrong*

Most people think success and failure are opposites, but they are products of the same process. American inventor Charles Kettering once said, "Virtually nothing comes out right the first time. Failures, *repeated* failures, are finger posts on the road to achievement...." After a mistake, wise people learn from it and avoid making the same error again.

Explorer Christopher Columbus erred while looking for a shorter route to India, and discovered the Americas. Inventor Thomas Edison knew 1,800 ways *not* to build a light bulb, yet he kept persisting and eventually succeeded.

We learn from trial and error, *not* by doing things the same way each time. If you are original in your approach, you will be wrong a lot of the time. It's a fact of life. *Progress always involves risk; you can't steal second base with one foot on first.* Remember the words of Dale Carnegie, "All life is a chance. So take it! The person who goes furthest is the one who is willing to do and dare."

Thomas Watson, the founder of IBM, said, "The way to succeed is to double your failure rate." If you make an error, use it as a stepping stone to a new idea you might not have otherwise discovered.

Strengthen your risk "muscle." Everybody has one, but you need to exercise it or it will atrophy. Take on risk, small or large, every day. For example, attend a personal growth workshop, call that prospect or client you've been afraid to call, interview a businessperson about their success strategies, or volunteer to give a presentation.

Mental Block 4—*Play Is Frivolous*

Play is actually essential. During what kinds of activities do you get your ideas?

- ♦ When you are faced with a problem?
- ♦ When things break down?
- ♦ When there is a need to fill?
- ♦ When you are having fun?
- ♦ When you are taking yourself lightly?
- ♦ When you wake up in the middle of the night?

- While you are exercising?
- During a long meeting?
- While you are showering or shaving?

Physicist Albert Einstein once said, "Make friends with your shower. If you are inspired to sing, maybe the song has an idea in it for you."

Play is inspirational, relaxes us, and helps our creative juices flow. Author Roger Von Oech wrote, "Necessity may be the mother of invention, but play is certainly the father." Your mental blocks are loosened during play. It allows you to go into your own imaginary world with the purpose of having fun. Children generally don't know all the "have to's" and "should's," and are unrestrained in their play. Plato wrote, "Life must be lived as play." Make your business and personal life as much fun as possible, and watch the creativity bubble up.

Mental Block 5—*I'm Not Creative*

We need to recognize our own talents and skills which we may have taken for granted in the past. They are usually the ones that bring out our creativity. Delivering an excellent presentation, decorating a lovely home, brainstorming for unique solutions, putting together a colorful wardrobe, telling wonderful stories, cooking delicious meals, planting a beautiful lawn and garden, keeping a family, department, or business coordinated and working effectively together (especially during challenging times), and writing interesting articles are just a few of the talents and skills people often take for granted.

If you say to yourself, "I can't do that!" you are either not thinking creatively or you may mean, "I don't want to do that." Decide what you would really like to do and picture what fun you'd have and the difference you would make. Let me get you started—dream of what you would really like to do with the rest of your life.

Successful athletes visualize themselves winning before the competition begins. They run a mental movie through their minds over and over. This creative way of "winning" beforehand, builds confidence. *There is tremendous power in your belief.* Your eyes are opened. Your opportunities become clear and, as you take action, your visions can become realities. When teams are in a slump, it is usually because they are reliving failures in their minds. How about you?

Here's a wonderful example of desire conquering defeat:

Two frogs fell into a bucket of cream. The first frog, seeing no way to get his footing in the thick white liquid, accepted his fate and drowned. The second frog didn't like that approach. He started thrashing around in the cream and doing whatever he could to stay afloat. After a while, all of this churning motion turned the cream into butter, and he was able to regain his footing and hop out!

Our creativity, or lack of it, can mean our survival. It makes the difference between having a variety-packed, rich, fulfilling life, or a dull existence where we get stuck in a rut of sameness. I choose to be creative. How about you?

Mental Block 6—*Don't Do Anything Different*

Candid Camera, a brilliant and funny U.S. television program aired this scene in 1960:

A man waits patiently for an elevator in an office building. When it arrives, the doors open. He notices that everyone is turned around, facing the inside. He steps in and faces the inside of the elevator too, with his back to the doors, even though there was no logical reason for doing so.

When we follow the masses of negative-thinking people, we get the same results they do, which is typically gray mediocrity. People who win venture out, lead the way, and create their own following.

Creative people maintain open, imaginative minds. Seeing the many possibilities, and how to achieve them, marks the power of imagination. Your imagination is your own personal laboratory. You can rehearse the almost endless possibilities, map out plans, and visualize overcoming obstacles. Imagination, plus follow-up action, turns possibilities into realities.

It takes courage to do something different—to risk criticism. If you're concerned about what others may be thinking of you—don't be. Most people aren't thinking about you—they're thinking about themselves!

To some, this may come as a rude awakening. If so, consider this fact of life as freeing yourself up to do what you need and want to do, as long as you're creating win-win situations. As was mentioned earlier, no one else pays your bills. You need to do what's right for you.

Dare to be different—drive on the road of creativity and adventure. You'll find like-minded people to travel with you.

Playwright George Bernard Shaw wrote, "You see things and you say, 'Why?' But I dream things that never were, and I say, 'Why not?'" American writer Louisa May Alcott wrote, "Far away, there in the sunshine, are my highest aspirations. I may not reach them, but I can look up and see their beauty, believe in them, and endeavor to follow where they lead."

Publisher Malcolm Forbes declared, "When you cease to dream, you cease to live." So continue to dream of what could be and follow the less traveled road, or create your own road, in your quest for a richly rewarding life. Many others have done so, and you can too!

Mental Block 7—*It's Not My Responsibility*

I hear this excuse throughout the business world. My question to those who say it is, "If it were your responsibility, what would you do?" Recall the last time you heard "That's not my department," or "That's not my job." What did it tell you about that person? They're certainly not service-oriented, are they? How would your associates feel if you said that to them, and then turned away? They surely wouldn't look to you for leadership, would they? They probably would think you don't care about them.

Some people may say, "Other people make decisions and take actions that affect me. I'm not responsible for everything that happens to me." While it's true that you're not responsible for other people's behavior, *you* are responsible for all your *responses* to other people's actions. You're responsible for your attitudes and actions. We all are. The question is, "How do you respond to your experiences?"

What "extra"—beyond what you believe you absolutely need to do—are you doing for others? The person who takes on something beyond the call of duty, who goes the extra mile, is exhibiting a leadership trait. They don't whine or complain. They jump in and do whatever it takes to get the job done. They're motivated by excellence and understand the importance of setting a good example for others to follow.

The responsibility for fulfillment of your dreams lies within you and you alone. You may get some support along the way, but the ultimate responsibility is yours. Don't expect the government, your neighbors, your friends, or even your spouse, to do it. It's up to you! When you understand and accept this, then nothing, or no one, can deny you your greatness. *The power to succeed or fail is yours. And no one can take that away from you.*

If you are excited about the new ideas you have read here, but fail to use them to change things in your life, *nothing* will happen and the ideas will vanish. A motivational expression I often hear is, "If it is to be, it's up to me." The day we take total responsibility for everything we do or don't do is a day of victory—the beginning of our true success.

Strive for Excellence

Excellence is a vital quality of people who achieve their personal and professional best. Excellence is going far beyond the call of duty—doing more than is expected. That's what differentiates those who excel and achieve their dreams and goals from those who don't. This includes maintaining the highest standards, looking after the smallest details, and going the extra mile. Do your absolute best so you can achieve the excellence you need to go *full speed ahead.*

U.S. Army General George Patton once said, "If a man has done his best, what else is there?" U.S. President Abraham Lincoln wrote, "I do the very best I know how, the very best I can, and I mean to keep on doing so until the end." And Thomas Edison shared, "If there is a way to do it better, find it."

Discover what your greatest talent is, then fully use it and you'll realize a level of satisfaction and triumph few people will ever know. If you conduct meetings at your job or in your business, how can you improve them and support your associates in being more creative?

Here are some ideas you can use to have energetic, uplifting, and results-oriented sessions:

♦ Make only positive statements.
♦ Listen to each other's experiences, discuss them, and learn from them.
♦ Role play with each other to learn new techniques.
♦ Never criticize, condemn, complain, or compare.
♦ Ask what has worked in the past.
♦ Do something you have never done before.
♦ Have a fresh, childlike approach.
♦ Add humor and fun.
♦ Get excited about doing whatever it takes.
♦ Think of constant improvement.
♦ Use enthusiasm-igniting phrases like: "Keep talking," "You're on the right track," "We can do it," "Wow! Let's do it!" "It's sure nice to have you with us," and "Look out world, here we come, *full speed ahead!*"
♦ Focus on your dreams.

Use these ideas to become more creative and reach your next level of success and to help your associates to do the same.

The more creative you are, the more you'll be on a never-ending adventure. It can take you places you've always dreamed of. It is fun to accomplish the difficult or the seemingly impossible; that is where there is less competition.

If at first you don't succeed, do it again, only better. Learn from your mistakes. If everyone says you're wrong, evaluate their reasoning. If you still believe you're right, keep going. If you believe they are partially right, fine-tune your approach accordingly, and keep persisting. If everyone laughs at you, consider it part of the scenery on your road of success, and laugh with them.

Develop a team of diverse, forward-thinking people and expand your focus from creative individual performance to group creation. No matter what, stay creative and keep going.

Creativity is a vital part of your road map for success. You don't need exceptional intelligence to be creative. It's simply a possibility-generating outlook—a set of skills and habits anyone can develop. Those who merely want to survive and just make a living, rather than make a life, don't need to be concerned about imagination and vision.

People who are committed to a joyful, fulfilling life of service will creatively stretch their imaginations and experience their dreams mentally. They'll keep them alive by continuing to picture them as they persevere to make them a reality. Each time they hit a new plateau of achievement they dream bigger and start the process over.

Make thoughtful, creative choices about your future. Don't let your future be the result of other people's choices. Others may not have your best interests at heart. Steer toward a future that is wonderful, exciting, happy, and most of all, full of creativity and realized dreams. Drive toward a bold new tomorrow. You'll be glad you did—it's worth the effort!

Now Implement the *Full Speed Ahead* Action Plan...

Start by reviewing the **Four Cs of Creativity.** They can help you accelerate on your road of success.

1. *Curiosity*—There is always the possibility for a better way! Play the "what if" game with a pen and a clean sheet of paper or on your computer screen. What if people were born old and grew young? What if people slept two hours and were awake 22 hours each day?

2. *Courage*—Someone once said, "Behold the turtle. He makes progress only when he sticks his neck out!" Courage means facing your fears while shifting gears into overdrive. Being creative means taking risks courageously. What smart risks have you taken recently? Write them down.

3. *Climate*—In your business or profession, in your community and at home, creativity can help you move on. Always

be on the lookout for improvement and share your ideas with your boss or leader, or implement them yourself if you're the boss, leader, or business owner.

If you are in business where you are associated with a network of people or are a part of a franchise where duplication is encouraged, it's likely you have a proven pattern of success to follow. You can be creative within these guidelines, and share with your mentor, leader, or corporate supplier(s) other inventive ideas to make positive changes.

How have you helped create a positive environment at home and in your business or place of employment? How could you make a greater difference in these areas? Write your thoughts down.

4. *Commitment*—List your most important business, career, and personal goals. Will you commit yourself to them? Will you do whatever it takes to carry them out—to make them happen?

There's a difference between interest and commitment. When you're just interested in doing something, you do it only when it's convenient. When you're *committed* to doing it, you accept no excuses, only results. As Ralph Waldo Emerson said, "There is no strong performance without a little fanaticism in the performer."

So go ahead and be creative. If you keep doing the same thing, you'll just keep getting the same result. What could you do differently to get what you want in all areas of your life? You'll be amazed at the positive changes you can make when you're committed, make creative decisions, and follow through with the necessary action until you've achieved what you set out to do!

Write down the new ideas for constant improvement you've learned from this chapter. Use them within 24 hours, if possible. Make a copy of this plan and place it in a prominent location in your home or office. Do the things you've made note of.

Top performers realize they need to constantly improve and keep their "engines" tuned-up. They realize that coasting only happens when going downhill and leads to a standstill. They know that being in neutral is stagnation, which is an indication of the need to change and grow. What are you doing differently today than you were one year ago? How do you constantly improve at home, on your job, or in your business?

Chapter 8

Risk-Taking and Goal-Setting—Create Your Own Road Map

*"Once you accept the hazards, take your focus off the risks,
concentrate on the goal, and remain positive."*
Joyce Weiss

You Need to Have a Dream and Go for It!

What is a dream? It is a fond hope, an aspiration, a vision of an ideal. What is a goal? It is an objective—a dream with a date on it. What is a risk? It is the chance of loss. These words play a role in everyone's life. When you have dreams and goals and take risks, it shows in the sparkle in your eyes, your smile, your high energy, and the bounce of your step. And if you don't, that also shows—in your boredom, lack of enthusiasm, and a low energy level.

Over the years I have consulted with many successful people about their careers. I ask them what advice they give to others just starting out. The simplicity of their answers is fascinating. They suggest:

♦ Take risks early on in your career or business.
♦ Have the courage to chase your dreams.

♦ Have a general plan of action and review it each year. Make sure you are headed in the right direction.

Taking risks and setting goals are topics that people talk a lot about yet many neglect to take the necessary action. This chapter will cover the importance of taking risks, why people fear risk, and how to find the courage to take more risks in order to excel in this fast-paced world. You will learn how to use goal-setting strategies to turn your dreams into magnificent realities.

Did you ever think about how a lobster grows when its shell is so hard? A lobster instinctively knows when its body is cramped and sheds its shell at regular intervals. Before it does, it finds a safe spot to rest while the hard shell comes off. During the process a soft pink membrane is exposed, before it eventually hardens into its next shell. Obviously, the lobster is vulnerable without its protective shell. It can be thrown against a coral reef or eaten by other sea creatures. The lobster risks its life to grow!

We can learn valuable lessons from lobsters—we, too, need to risk in order to grow and change. People know when their shells have grown too tight. They become angry, frightened, bored, stifled, or find life very dull. They move along, in a survival mode, just grinding their gears, continuing to smother in their old shells, no longer productive. They may feel safe, but rarely does anything new ever happen to them. And if it does, it's usually someone else's choice, not theirs. Therefore, it may not be in their best interest.

Some people have a greater understanding of the nature of fine-tuning themselves to live the life they want. To the unaware, they seem to be luckier. But, in truth, they're making their own luck. They consistently take action toward the realization of their goals and dreams. To grow, they realize they need to shed their shells of complacency and take risks. With risk comes vulnerability. I invite you to shed last year's shell—despite the potential challenges associated with it—and get ready for new, exciting adventures.

Actor Alan Alda said to his daughter, "Be brave enough to live creatively. Your creativity is a place no one else has ever been. You need to leave the city of your comfort. Go into the wilderness of doing what you feel inspired to do. You can't get there by bus, only by hard work and risk, and by not quite knowing what you're doing. What you'll discover will be wonderful. What you'll discover will be yourself."

Why do people fear taking risks? What keeps them stuck in their routines? Let's take a look at six risk busters:

Habits and Comfort—*The First Risk Buster*

People are often bound by habits and comfort. They may feel they have no control and perhaps don't even realize they *are* capable of change. They are often negative-thinking and usually surround themselves with people who think like them—rather than positive-thinking people who would encourage them to follow their dreams.

Such people focus on the challenges rather than the solutions. They view themselves as stuck and say such things as:

- I am too old (too young).
- My skills are not up to date.
- I am not happy in this line of work, but at least it's a job—it pays the bills.
- I'll never be rich.

Unfortunately, many people shut themselves down and limit their vision with these negative messages. Sometimes it takes a life-changing event, like being laid off from their job, a serious illness, or a peer dying, to give them a wake-up call. This causes people to stop and think about what they're doing. They realize they need to make some changes, because they're not going to live forever.

Must and Should—*The Second Risk Buster*

Others resist change because they follow the "must" and "should" rules, like "Everyone in my family is a teacher. I should follow in their footsteps." Using these words may show our guilt for not doing what we think is expected of us. A workshop participant once said, "I tell people not to 'should' on me."

"Shoulding" on people puts them in boxes and stifles their creativity. Instead of saying, "You must...," or "You should...," say "You could...." This liberates others to be creative and do what is best for them.

Fear of Making Mistakes—*The Third Risk Buster*

People don't take risks because they're afraid of looking foolish or making mistakes. The pain of change may appear to be greater than the pain of staying the same. However, when the pain of staying the same exceeds the *perceived* pain of making the change, most people make the decision to move on.

Many individuals don't understand that successful people make lots of mistakes on the way to reaching their goals. Every artist spoils many canvases. Every accountant uses the delete key on the computer and a pencil with an eraser. No baseball player ever had a batting average of 1000.

People who win don't allow their mistakes to stop them. Instead, they learn from them—what *not* to do! The person who rarely makes a mistake is the person who rarely accepts challenges. They lead a life of boring sameness. He or she merely survives and never thrives. Is that what you really want? Take a chance on yourself and go for it—*full speed ahead.* You're worth it!

Unresolved Personal Challenges—*The Fourth Risk Buster*

People are often stymied in their personal or professional and business life because they don't resolve the personal challenges that make them unhappy. They complain about people and situations, yet they don't take full responsibility for their lives. And they don't work to improve things. You *can* learn how to communicate more effectively, be more persistent, and overcome procrastination. And you can learn all the other skills you need to be effective on the road of success.

Of course, it's easier to complain and accept the stance of a victim than to accept responsibility. But in the long-run, you are doomed to experience long-term pain and dissatisfaction. It is easier to blame someone else than to examine patterns in our own behavior that hinder our success.

One gentleman complained that he always marries the wrong kind of woman. He recently married for the eighth time! I suggested he look within for patterns in his choice of wives. He was not open to my suggestion; he would rather continue to play the blame game. Until he accepts the need to change his thinking and behavior, he is destined to repeat his old mistakes.

This is true for all of us. This is a cause-and-effect world. It's really quite simple. We just need to stop and examine what we're doing that is giving us poor results.

This is part of being alive and doing whatever it takes to be successful in our endeavors whether we like it or not. The people who win invest time in self-examination and learn new ways of thinking and behaving. And they do this as many times as it takes to achieve their goal or dream.

Fear of the Unknown—*The Fifth Risk Buster*

It's likely we've all heard and used some of the following excuses at one time or another:

- ◆ I don't have time.
- ◆ I'm not ready yet.
- ◆ I don't have the money.
- ◆ I might fail.
- ◆ When the children grow up, I'll do it.
- ◆ I don't know enough.
- ◆ I know (<u>name</u>) lost money doing this.
- ◆ Someday, when I have everything in order, I will make the change.
- ◆ I don't know anybody.

Do you remember your first day of living in a new community? What about your first day of camp, high school or college, or at a new job? You were probably scared. But you were also excited and full of anticipation, weren't you?

Conquering other fears feels much the same. You need to gear yourself up to make a change. Tell yourself, "I can handle anything that comes my way." This helps you to prepare yourself to walk into unfamiliar territory and leave behind your safe, reliable, comfort zone. Remember, *action cures fear.*

Fear is a part of growing. We will always fear the new and unknown to varying degrees, as long as we're stretching and growing. Look back at what you feared one, five, or ten years ago. Do most of those fears seem small and trivial today? Are some of them still plaguing you? Do you need to shift gears to overcome those fears? If so, you are not alone.

For some people, the fear of failure is worse than the fear of death. If you need to worry about something, think of the opportunities you'll miss if you don't conquer the fear. One good thing about failure is that it inspires no jealousy! Most everyone can relate to that! Our failures are there to learn from and keep us human.

British poet Rudyard Kipling wrote, "We have forty million reasons for failure, but not a single excuse." Some people have thousands of excuses why they can't do something, when all they need is one reason why they need to do it. *If something is worth doing, it is worth doing poorly on the first attempt, and on every attempt, until you get it right.*

Lack of Support—*The Sixth Risk Buster*

Lack of support is another reason why some people are stuck in neutral. They don't have unconditional loving support from others who believe in them. They're often associating with people who are also stuck. They need to find someone to talk to who is at the level of success where they want to be, who'll cheer them on.

They don't know what to do because they haven't brainstormed with other successful people. We need the power that comes with meeting and associating with other positive-thinking people.

This one ingredient can mean the difference between having low octane or high octane fuel in your tank. This is key to developing the necessary understanding and skills to reach each new destination on your road of success.

To reach a new goal or dream, it takes a new level of awareness. You never reach this awareness at the old level of thinking.

You need encouragement and teaching from people who have met their aspirations.

To keep up the momentum, you'll want to go *full speed ahead* to a new level of thinking! Many success stories begin because that person talked with positive-thinking people who shared how they overcame their challenges. Additional energy can be ignited by reading positive books, viewing motivational and inspiring videos, listening to educational audio tapes, and attending up-beat seminars.

On the Road of Excellence

What methods can you use when you want to excel? The first step is to recognize obstacles you may be placing in you own path. Then share the risk busters with others who are having difficulty breaking their patterns of fear and failure.

Colonel Harlan Sanders was 65 years old when he opened his first Kentucky Fried Chicken outlet. He had just received his first retirement check when he decided upon this new venture. He assumed everyone loved fried chicken, so he went about sharing his idea with others. His concept didn't work at first; 1009 restaurant people were not interested! Did that stop him? Number 1010 said yes, and the rest is history. KFC has become a world-renowned success story.

Some people think every new idea has to be dramatic, such as sky diving or mountain climbing. This isn't so. Whether you seek a promotion, would like to meet someone new, move to another location, or start a new business, all new ideas involve at least a small amount of risk.

The more you understand the art of risk-taking, the better able you will be to take smarter risks. Consider it an adventure, no matter what happens, and you'll be on the right road! Be confident, yet not attached to the outcome.

Here are five stages of risk-taking you can use to make intelligent choices, as you strive to make your dream come true. It might be helpful to discuss this in the company of a positive-thinking, supportive family member, friend, or with a mentor or leader who's encouraging you on your road of success.

Risk-Taking Stage 1—*Choose a Dream and Make It a Goal*
Select a dream you want to achieve. Give it a target date, and turn it into a goal. This is a powerful strategy that helps you achieve the things you want. Picture its completion, in as much detail as possible. Write down your target date and the description of what you want. Include all the details. To get you started, here are some potential goals:

♦ Travel across the U.S. in a motor home during the summer of_____.

♦ Buy a new fishing boat by_____.

♦ Double my business or professional income by _____.

♦ Increase my number of business associates to_____by _____.

♦ Travel to Europe for a month with my family the summer of _____.

♦ Go to the achievement or promotional level of _____ in my business or career by the end of the fiscal year.

♦ Build my dream home by_____.

♦ Play golf on seven of the best golf courses of the world, one a year for the next seven years, starting on _____.

♦ Sail around the world by_____.

♦ Walk the ten most beautiful beaches of the world, one a year, in the next ten years.

♦ Become a healthy 150 pounds by June 1st.

♦ Enrich my marriage by communicating with my spouse one solid, uninterrupted half-hour a day at 5:30 p.m. on Tuesday, Thursday, and Saturday.

♦ Give myself time to do whatever I want; get up 45 minutes earlier than my family on Tuesday, Thursday, and Saturday.

♦ Firm my muscles, strengthen my heart, and increase my energy level by taking a brisk half-hour walk every day.

Risk-Taking Stage 2—*Prepare and Plan for Risk*
Fear helps you to prepare. It's important to confront the unknown at this time. You can't change any part of your life you aren't willing to face—it's that simple. So ask yourself, "What or

whom am I allowing to hold me back?" "Is it my spouse?" "My mother or father?" "A relative or friend?" "The fact that I'm such a busy person?" Remember, no person or thing can hold you back without your permission! You are the one in the driver's seat of your life.

If you're trying not to "rock the boat," trying to please others to get their stamp of approval, or letting the fear of rejection get in the way, you need to face and overcome these challenges as you embark on something new. Avoid associating with others who feel they would be negatively affected by your changes.

As "Mr. No Excuse!" Jay Rifenbary teaches, "What happens to you, happens for you." When you get rebuttals from others, deal with them quickly, as you move toward your goals. This can help you strengthen your conviction, as you gear up to shift lanes on your highway of success. What really matters is that you believe in your heart that what you're doing is right for you and your family for the long-haul.

There may be some discomfort and uncertainty as you shift gears and take on a new role. Your job is to face it, deal with it, and keep on traveling. People who win on the road of success continue and persevere—no matter what detours they face.

Preparation and planning time offers you a great opportunity to assess potential losses. Accept that you could experience an upset. What specifically might you be afraid of losing? Is it security or money? Is it relationships or something else?

Get out a sheet of paper and draw a line down the middle. On the left side, list the possible benefits of reaching your goal. On the right side, list the potential losses or negatives you may experience. Do the positives outweigh the negatives? What's the absolute worst thing, in your estimation, that could happen? Are you willing to accept that possibility? If not, you'll probably want to rethink your dreams and perhaps choose another goal.

In your decision-making process it may be helpful to discuss your situation with a supportive mentor who can guide you. You may be scared and sabotaging your own success with negative ideas. Perhaps this coach could help you be more objective and therefore make a better decision for you and your family. You'll want to ask yourself, and perhaps this mentor, "If I go ahead now, how can I limit my losses? How could I get out of the situation, if necessary, before the worst happens?"

When you get to the point where you can accept the worst thing that could happen by taking the risk, you are ready to move on to the next stage. Once you accept the hazards, take your focus off the risks, concentrate on the goal, and remain positive! What you aim for can become a self-fulfilling prophecy.

Risk-Taking Stage 3—*Develop a Plan of Action*

Let's say your goal is to start building your dream home in 24 months. You've been working hard in your business or career and your efforts are starting to pay off. You've been diligently doing what it takes and your momentum of success is increasing. You've attracted and trained some key people who are leadership material and they are starting to produce great results. You've even gone high-tech because your products and services are available through e-commerce to millions of people.

You've got the dreambuilding pictures of the house you want posted throughout your home—on your refrigerator, on your bathroom mirror, in your family room, and in your office—to reinforce your dream. Underneath each picture you have a positive statement in the present tense, "We love living in our beautiful white two-story French country home."

Both of these approaches—posting the photos and affirming your dream as reality—help you to create a new comfort level with your dream. It becomes a familiar part of your everyday life. It's then easier for you to take the necessary risks and persist until you reach your treasured goal. But there are still some missing pieces of the puzzle to your actually going from Point A, the comfortable home you're living in now which is not your dream home, to Point B, the home you really want.

So what's between you and building your dream house—a breathtaking white brick home with expansive windows and peaks that seem to touch the sky? The golf course across the street from your house calls your name so loudly, you can't help but hear it. So you put your "thinking cap" on. You take out a sheet of paper and start brainstorming with your mentor and your spouse to determine what you need to do:

1. Triple your business or career sales volume.
2. Pay off the car loans.
3. Sell the motorcycle, which isn't being used anyway.
4. Help your three children prepare to qualify for sports and academic scholarships—to pay for college.
5. Pay off your mortgage.
6. Practice delayed gratification rather than indulge in impulse purchases.
7. Pay off your three credit cards.
8. Involve the children in the process.

You take each one of these things and break them down into action steps and goal dates. You make big charts on poster board and tape them to the wall.

Your commitment is unwavering. Each month you meet with your mentor, your spouse, and your children, to discuss the progress you are making toward your dream house. You adjust your goals as you go, knowing that a delay isn't a denial. For example, you discover that getting your finances in order takes three-and-a-half years before you're able to start building. It's worth it to be in a solid financial position so you can truly enjoy your new home.

You worked together as a family team with the guidance of your mentor, and the process has been challenging. You all grew through it together. Moving day is a big victory and you celebrate at a local restaurant, toasting each other and laughing.

Your youngest daughter looks at you and your spouse, with a twinkle in her eye, "Well, Mom and Dad, we're getting pretty good at this dream stuff. What are we going to do next?" Before you have a chance to answer, you son pipes up, "Hey, let's take a trip to Disney World next year!" Their confidence is strong and healthy and you know you're gearing up for another adventure.

Risk-Taking Stage 4—*Make a Commitment to Take Risks*

This is the point of no return—putting your plan into action. No more just talking about it. It's time to put the pedal to the metal and go for it—*full speed ahead.*

The *American Heritage Dictionary* defines commitment as—"the state of being bound emotionally or intellectually to a course of action." It's doing whatever it takes to reach your goal or dream. When you're committed, you accept no excuses from yourself or anyone else. You persistently go after what you want, regardless of the challenges along the road.

Risk-Taking Stage 5—*Evaluate Your Plan and Results*

You've completed your plan of action. You broke away from the old patterns of doing things and creatively moved forward. You dared to be different, to reach beyond the old levels of accomplishment, stepping boldly into tomorrow. You took the risk, now let's evaluate it.

Courage Comes When You Take Action

We examined the importance of taking risks. Now how can you get the courage to take more risks? Keep in mind what Helen Keller once said, "...avoiding danger is no safer in the long-run than outright exposure. Life is either a daring adventure or nothing." Every time you take action toward your goal or dream you gain experience. This makes you stronger and more courageous, and increases your confidence.

Every time you confront your fear, even though there may be risks, you prove to yourself that you can win on the road of success and drive your vehicle to the summit of the mountain. If your engine sputters and stops along the way, do whatever it takes to get it started again, regain your momentum, and get back on the road to your dreams and goals.

Have the courage to go the first mile. Getting started is half the challenge. Once you get into motion, it's easier to keep moving forward. Take one day at a time. Success is never final and failure can be your greatest teacher. It's your courage that counts. Be a role model for others to follow!

A well-known newspaper columnist said, "Expect challenges as an inevitable part of life. When they come, keep the crown of your head high, face them head-on and pronounce, 'I am stronger than you. I will defeat you.'"

We've all heard stories about people overcoming great obstacles in their lives, whether they are about a physical illness or personal challenge. Success can be attributed to focusing on your dream or goal, courage, strength, hope, and persistent action—despite the odds.

Mark Twain once wrote, "Courage is resistance to fear, master of fear, not absence of fear." Remember, success does not come to *you*. You go to *it*. "What you are afraid to do is a clear indicator of the next thing you need to do," a wise person once offered.

Quotes like these have helped many people to stay on course, especially when things looked bleak. Use index cards to capture some of the quotations throughout this book. Carry them with you or display them on your refrigerator, mirror, or desk, and share them with your family, friends, and associates to encourage them too. Inspirational quotes reinforce the idea that you need courage to take risks, no matter what the outcome may be. Fortunately, things usually turn out better than we imagine. But, nonetheless, it takes courage, patience, and faith to do what we need to do to achieve the results we want.

British playwright George Bernard Shaw wrote, "The people who get on in this world are the people who get up and look for the circumstances they want, and if they can't find them, they make them." And Victor Hugo shared, "People don't lack strength; they lack will." *Taking risks separates people who just survive day-to-day from those who do their personal best to achieve their dreams and goals.*

Take a Risk a Day!

Remember to put the five stages of risk-taking ideas into action. Go out on the limb—that's where the fruit is.

Most people go through their days doing pretty much the same types of maintenance activities. And they aren't successful! They tend to stay on the same straight and narrow road until they wear a rut into it.

Whereas, the person with success habits takes the road rarely traveled and may even make their own road. How can you be counted as one of those fortunate few? Would you like to have more adventure in your life? Practice being adventurous by taking a risk a day!

Have you been afraid to call a potential client or prospect? Call them! Have you been putting off asking them for their business or to associate with you? Do it! Pick at least one small risk a day, and challenge yourself to do it. Then watch your courage and confidence grow!

The only way you can make a change is by taking a risk. You're in the driver's seat. No one else wants to achieve your dreams like you do. No one else will get fired up about making your vision come true. Take charge and make it happen!

Show others you're serious. You take the lead—the initiative. You may be surprised how others will support you. But even if they don't, the steering wheel is in your hands. It's still your responsibility.

Rather than wait for someday, do it today! Even if you're afraid, do it anyway—*take that risk!*

Now get out a sheet of paper, make a list of at least five things you have failed to do because of the fear of risk, and describe that risk. Your list may look somewhat like this:

1. Call Bob and share the idea of his joining you as an associate in your business. Bob is a respected professional in your community and you've been afraid to approach him.
2. Call the realtor who is showing your dream house and ask him or her for a tour. Request that they take pictures of you and your family in front of the house. You've been afraid that the realtor wouldn't give you much attention because you believe you can't afford this house—not yet, anyway.
3. Go to your local car dealer and take a test-drive of that new red sports car you've been wanting. You've been concerned that your spouse would criticize you if you pursued your car dream.
4. Ask your friends if they would be willing to babysit your toddler for the weekend while you and your spouse go to a motivational seminar. You've never been to such a seminar. You're also not familiar with the location where it's being held. You don't know what to expect.

5. Ask your boss for a promotion and the raise you believe you deserve, and say why you deserve it based on what you have done and can do for the company. You've believed for months now that you deserve a raise or a promotion, but have been avoiding talking to your boss about it.

Tape the list to your bathroom mirror or any place where you will see it every day. Check these items off as you do them. Then make another list of five and repeat the process. You may find this will keep you excited and you'll get accustomed to taking risks.

Most everything you ever did that proved to be worthwhile caused you to risk. Have you ever moved to a new location, gone to a new school, learned to drive a car, joined a new organization, got a new job, made new friends, talked to a new prospect or customer, bought a house, or got married?

All those experiences represent taking a risk. You may have been afraid as you ventured forward. But you proceeded anyway. You've already proved to yourself and others that you can successfully take risks.

Putting your goals into action by taking the necessary risks is "where the rubber meets the road." It's great to have goals. But there's a *big* difference between people who say the words and those who put their words into action.

A good example of this is a story about Mary who had just met George. As he opened the door for her, she said, "You look like my husband."

George commented, "I didn't realize you were married." Mary smiled and said, "I'm not!"

This woman knew how to dream, was motivated, and put her thoughts into action. Mary had all the right qualities for successful goal-setting.

Do You Have a Burning Desire and an Unrelenting Commitment?

Many talented individuals fail because they lack the intense desire and strong commitment it takes to make their dreams a reality. They may write out their goals but aren't dedicated and don't take action. Their goals remain just wishes. Without desire and action, nothing much happens. We all need strong desire and commitment so we can hurdle over the obstacles to reach our goals.

Many victories have been snatched by the person with less talent and skills—simply because he or she had more desire to win. Their risk-taking and persistence got them there. When you are committed to taking action in the direction of your dream, everything stands within your reach. As Walt Disney, animator and film producer, told us, *"All of our dreams can come true if we have the courage to pursue them."*

Having a great desire and a solid commitment fuels our courage. Abraham Lincoln said, *"Always bear in mind that your own resolution to succeed is more important than any other one thing."* The truly motivated person knows that overcoming obstacles is a necessary part of implementing any game plan. Anyone who believes there will be no bumps or detours on their road of success will surely be surprised. As long as you have a burning desire to do something and an unrelenting commitment, you *will* find a way to get it done. You will become one of those people who reaches their destination.

Opportunity Is All Around You

An important key in reaching your goals and dreams is the ability to see opportunity everywhere. There are no limits to our opportunities. Most of us see only a small portion of what is possible. Opportunities are created by seeing the possibilities, and having the courage to act on them. Opportunities are always there—we just need to look for them.

English essayist Samuel Johnson said, "To improve the golden moment of opportunity, and catch the good that is within our reach, is the great art of life." Thomas Edison wrote, "Opportunity is missed by most people because it is dressed in overalls and looks like work." A challenge is often an opportunity to plant seeds of progress. We need to turn obstacles into opportunities to grow and become the best we can be. Albert Einstein said, "In the middle of difficulty is opportunity."

It takes effort to discover the gift of opportunity during challenging times but, when you sincerely and open-mindedly look for it, it will appear. Remember—*the magic inside you is no hocus pocus. Set your goals and you create the focus.* Knowing where you're headed will help you find the diamond of opportunity hidden in the chunk of coal.

What Is Your Focus?

The purpose of setting goals is to focus your attention. Your mind cannot focus until it has clear objectives. Otherwise, it's like a car rolling down the road without a driver, swerving this way and that, directed by the bumpy road, and eventually crashing.

The magic begins when you set goals. It starts your engine. Goals give you a destination to aim for and scenic guideposts along the way to tell you you're on the right road. You step on the gas and begin to accelerate, as you keep a watchful eye on your next goal.

You realize that nature has bestowed you with all the power you need to accomplish your goals. This may come in the form of people, resources, ideas, or something else. "People with goals succeed because they know where they are going," observed Earl Nightingale, professional speaker. Do you know where *you* are going?

What Do You Really, Really Want?

An important step in getting what you want out of life is to decide exactly what you want. (Read that again!) If you haven't been getting what you want, you may need to define it more precisely. There may be fog on your windshield, making it difficult to see ahead and stay on the road. A hazy idea of what you want leads to hazy results. Whereas, a clearly defined desire helps you steer your vehicle in the right direction and keeps you driving, until you reach your destination.

When I worked as a guidance counselor, I dealt with people who wanted to change careers. Those who came in with clear-cut ideas about what they wanted to do had the most success. When someone walked in saying, "I will do anything, just find me a job!" I knew it would be a much bigger challenge to place this client in a satisfying position. They gave me no starting point because they honestly didn't know how important it was to identify a specific goal.

Helen Keller once shared, "True happiness...is not attained through self-gratification but through fidelity to a worthy purpose." Believe in the beauty of your dreams and goals and you'll be a building block for the future—yours and humankind's. Follow your heart because that's where the seeds of your potential are planted.

These insightful words from Lewis Carroll's *Alice in Wonderland* ring true. Alice asked the Cat, "Would you tell me, please, which way I ought to go from here?" "That depends a good deal on where you want to get to," said the Cat. "I don't much care where..." said Alice. "Then it doesn't matter which way you go," said the Cat. "...so long as I get *somewhere*," Alice added as an explanation. "Oh, you're sure to do that," said the Cat, "if you only walk long enough."

Here is a simple outline for putting your ideas into action:

Analysis—What do you really, really want? What's your dream? Discuss this with your spouse, a supportive friend, or your mentor.

Goals—Identify the specific goals you want to achieve. These can include challenges you need to face and overcome in your business, profession, personal life, or opportunities you want to pursue.

Ideas—Generate as many ideas and solutions as possible which could help you meet your goals. Include how you could team up with others to create win-win situations.

Selection—Analyze, identify, and select the ideas which are most likely to help you achieve your goals.

Action—Implement those selected ideas and make them reality. Don't concern yourself with knowing exactly what to do—when you have a big enough dream, you'll figure out the how-to along the way. Get yourself in motion and keep building momentum from there toward the realization of your goals.

Walk Your Talk

My son Ron often tells me, "I'm not just here for the ride. I'm here to drive." He is always challenging himself by doing such interesting things as running a marathon, scuba diving, or becoming a licensed airplane pilot. He walks his talk.

We all know people who simply exist. They go through the motions of getting through their days, exerting as little effort as possible. Yet, when we open our eyes and look, we notice there are so many exciting experiences available to us in life. We need to *seize the day*. As former automotive executive Lee Iacocca said in one of his Chrysler commercials, "Do something. Lead, follow, or get out of the way." And Rita Jones, my marketing genius, repeats an old saying, "Good things happen to those who wait. Great things happen to those who get out of their chair and go for it!"

Here are some questions I use in my workshops. To help stir you into action toward reaching your goals, ask yourself:

- Where do I want to be in one year; three years; five years?
- What do I need to do to get there?
- What risks do I need to take?
- What is the best possible outcome?

Define Your Dreams in a Simple Positive Statement

We talked about creating positive, present tense statements to reinforce your dream in your mind. Think and act positively; this could make the difference in your success. Negative thinking and behavior hinders you in your quest for your dreams. Now is the time to create a positive statement that defines your goals. State them as if they have already happened and are already a part of your reality, such as:

- I weigh 125 pounds and I feel in control.
- My wife (or husband) and I communicate clearly and lovingly.
- I am now a sales leader in my company and feel very good about the contribution I'm making.

◆ My appointment book is full. I enjoy building my business (or career), being out of debt and financially responsible. I am prepared for the future.

Repeat these statements over and over throughout your day, especially if you're facing an unpleasant situation. Write them on 3"×5" cards and display them in several prominent places. Let them be your affirmation to reflect your joyous anticipation of what's down the road for you. Don't be fooled by the simplicity of this. Things don't have to be complicated to be effective. Even if it seems silly or hopeless at first, stick with it. As you consistently say your positive statement(s) and take action toward the goals you've set, they will become a new reality. It will be a natural, inevitable progression.

A final thought on goal-setting: Be careful what you ask for; you'll probably get it. So be sure it's what you want! What we become is far more important than what we get in the process of being successful. Wouldn't it be great, when it's all said and done, to be able to honestly say, "I've become the kind of person I wanted to be"? What a positive thought. Let that be your ultimate outcome, and be encouraged as you grow and develop toward that pinnacle of achievement.

Go for Simplicity

It is important to look at our lives as simply as possible. For example, how you would answer the following question: What can you use to brush your teeth with, sleep on, and sit on? If you answered a toothbrush, a bed, and a chair, you answered correctly. Those who tried to think of one item for all three were making it more complicated than it needed to be!

We often live our lives more complexly than we need to. People are realizing this more and more and are simplifying their lives. Have a clear idea of what you want, what you're going to do to accomplish it, and methodically, day-by-day, focus on it and head in that direction.

People who achieve their personal best know one thing for sure: The magic to follow their dreams is within themselves. Those who wait for their future to come to them will find it wrapped up in other people's dreams, based on other people's agendas. Successful people go out and *create* their future, molding it from the dreams they found in their heart. Know that you can do virtually anything and everything you set your mind to. You *can* go *full speed ahead* toward your dreams. The question is: Will you?

Here are some ideas to keep in mind as you drive toward your dreams:

♦ Channel stress into positive energy.
♦ Gain control of your life.
♦ Accept full responsibility for your life. It's up to you to make your life better. It's up to you to respond to your experiences and to become the person you want to be.
♦ Take your life seriously and yourself a little lighter. Learn to laugh—especially in challenging situations.
♦ Communicate openly and confidently to earn the respect you deserve.
♦ Appreciate your uniqueness and the differences in others.
♦ Use your creativity at home, and in your business or profession, to discover the "magic" of your potential.
♦ Take more smart risks.
♦ Set your goals.
♦ Turn your dreams into magnificent realities.

At his inaugural address, the late U.S. President John F. Kennedy said, "All this will not be finished in the first 100 days. Nor will it be finished in the first 1,000 days, nor in the life of this administration, nor even perhaps in our lifetime on this planet. But let us begin."

We cannot always control what goes on around us but, with some thoughtful effort, we *can* control how we *respond* to what we experience. I challenge you to go beyond your comfort zone and have the courage to make mistakes, learn, laugh, and grow. Live your dreams. Others are doing it and you can too.

My dream for you is to continue going *full speed ahead!*

Now Implement the *Full Speed Ahead* Action Plan...

Creating change in our lives is often a challenging but, nonetheless, rewarding task. You'll most likely have a number of obstacles to overcome or work around before you can achieve your personal and business or career goals. This approach is designed to help you get in touch with some of the things you would like to change about yourself, what your new goals might be, and some of the risks, constraints, and consequences involved. The following outlines the steps you need to take:

From Here ➜	To There	Risks/Constraints Consequences
A	B	C

- ◆ In window A, draw a picture of something you would like to change about yourself.
- ◆ In window B, draw a picture of what you would like to be after the change.
- ◆ In window C, draw a picture of a barrier or constraint which might stand in your way, and a risk or consequence which might be involved, when you actually go *full speed ahead* to make the change.
- ◆ On a sheet of paper, list the actions you will take to overcome the challenge you drew in window C.

Now answer these five questions and take action:

1. Where do I want to be in five years?
2. What do I need to do to reach that goal?

3. What risks do I need to take?
4. What is the best thing that could happen to me?

Make a copy of your plan to move *full speed ahead* and place it in a prominent location in your home or office. Make sure you do all of the things you have made note of.

Are You on a Continuing Education Program?

Top performers are people who realize that lifelong learning is the only way to stay fresh and motivated. They invest in their own growth and development because they know that in order for their business or career to grow, they need to grow themselves first.

List the ways you stay motivated and grow. What books, tapes, seminars, conventions, or classes do you need to avail yourself of? Do you have a book of the month, weekly tapes, or other regularly scheduled activities that you can take advantage of? What continuing education activities and tools would you recommend to others?

Remember, build people to build your business or career. Whether you're leading or want to lead, you need to be on a continuing education program.

And whatever you do, get out there and do it! Shift into overdrive, put your pedal to the metal, and go...

Full Speed Ahead!

About the Author

Joyce Weiss, M.A., CSP (Certified Speaking Professional) is known as The Corporate Energizer®. She has conducted training in excellence workshops for 18 years, facilitating positive change with her enthusiasm and expertise. Joyce is known for her ability to help her clients create an energized and more productive team. Her diverse clients include: The American Hospital Association, Electronic Data Systems, Ford Motor Company, Ameritech, Hilton Hotels, and the Internal Revenue Service. She received her M.A. in Guidance and Counseling from Oakland University.

Joyce is a member of the Association for Quality and Participation, Meeting Professionals International, and the National Speakers Association which granted her a Certified Speaking Professional designation in 1993. She is among the few professional speakers (200 out of 4000 nationally and one out of only 50 women) who have earned this distinguished title.

She enjoys bike riding, photography, and learning new magic tricks to emphasize a point during her workshops. Joyce and her husband Jerry reside in West Bloomfield, Michigan. You may contact Joyce by phone at 248-681-5831, visit her website at www.joyceweiss.com, e-mail her at JoyceWeiss@aol.com, fax 248-682-0358, or write to: Joyce Weiss, M.A., CSP, The Corporate Energizer®, P.O. Box 250163, West Bloomfield, MI 48325-0163.